Notes from the Garden

Notes

from the

Garden

Creating a Pacific Northwest Sanctuary

by Madeleine Wilde

Edited by Mike Dillon

Foreword by David Streatfield

Illustrations by Mark Hinshaw

CHATWIN BOOKS

Seattle, 2021

Contents

Summer

Autumn

WINTER

*To Madeleine
and her extraordinary spirit*

Madeleine Wilde: At Home in the World

an Introduction by Mike Dillon

ON MAY 20, 2018, A WARM SUNDAY AFTERNOON, an interesting crowd filled the University of Washington Club to honor the life of Madeleine Wilde. The Seattle writer, gardener, gourmand, classical music aficionado, serious book reader, world traveler, and community activist died three months earlier after a brave fight against a rare form of lymphoma. Madeleine was seventy-four.

Two centuries ago, English poet and artist William Blake wrote: "The tree which moves some to tears of joy is in the Eyes of others only a Green thing that stands in the way."

Safe to say, those in the crowd that day did not look upon trees as green things that stand in the way. Madeleine's stance in life was reflected by those who turned out to honor her: friends, admirers of her writing, community activists, her own colleagues, and the colleagues of her husband, David Streatfield.

David, British born, is professor emeritus in the department of Landscape Architecture, University of Washington, and author of the much-honored *California Gardens: Creating a New Eden.*

I saw and met people of all ages and accomplishments that afternoon. Still, in my eyes, a common thread emerged: I can only call it a respect for the life of the mind and the work of the hands. These were classic Northwesterners who live in the world with a sense of stewardship and who, like Madeleine, train a fundamentally democratic lens, with a small "d," on life.

As one of seven people who took to the podium to speak, I read several excerpts from Madeleine's newspaper columns, "Notes from the Garden," which ran for two decades in the *Queen Anne & Magnolia News*, starting in the early 1990s.

I was Madeleine's publisher at Pacific Publishing Co. for most of that time. The News was the flagship paper in our group of community newspapers in Seattle, when the newspaper world was on firmer footing than it is now. We featured a stable of strong freelance writers and staffers, some of whom had contributed to *The Village Voice*, *The New York Times*, MSNBC, *The Seattle Times*, and other venues.

Writing from her garden on Queen Anne's southwest slope—one of Seattle's most beautiful neighborhoods—Madeleine's voice stood out. Over the years, I urged Madeleine to gather her columns into a book manuscript. In the last weeks of her life, she asked me to complete the job.

The garden, Madeleine often said, is a metaphor for the world. Madeleine's columns might deliver detailed advice on mulching one week and insights into the aesthetic pleasures of creating water islands the next.

She was not shy about sharing her love for certain gardening books or reminding us there is a proper way to stack a woodpile (do it "right"). A column on the art of raking touches base with Van Gogh rhapsodizing on the colors in the sky. Madeleine's prose, at times employing a canny wit, moves fluently between the practical and poetic.

Moments of Blakean wonder would occur. An April 1999 column reminds us how revelation waits in the lineaments of the familiar:

> *The garden continues to come to life, with the spring bulbs in full glory under deciduous trees filled with tender new leaves. There is a sense of a grand unfolding and nothing represents this better than the sword fern crosiers that are lifting their heads skyward. These new fern leaves are often also called fiddleheads, and are the edible part of the fern plant. Each day brings greater emergence, as the crosiers unfurl in scroll-like fashion. There is no riotous color to attract the eye, so why the intense fascination? For me, they evoke a sense of the primeval, the unfolding, the unbending, the loosening of a beginning.*

Madeleine was born in Pasadena, California, on February 27, 1943, and grew up in the Bay Area within a privileged, cultured family environment. The headstrong rebel of the family said goodbye to all that. After earning her degree in social science at the University of California, Santa Barbara, she headed for New York City and entered the brave new world of computer programming.

Madeleine returned to the Bay Area in the 1970s and continued her computer programming work. She also took an extension course at the University of California, Berkeley, where she immersed herself in garden design and building. The young woman from an upper-middle class family bent her back and got her hands dirty.

After moving to Seattle in the late 1970s, she met David, who was teaching at the University of Washington. In 1986 they bought a beautiful old house, built in 1911, on Queen Anne's steeply pitched southwest slope. To risk understatement, the house had seen better days. The couple, over the years, reclaimed the house and cleared the brambles to make way for their garden.

It is a woodland garden, a diverse micro-universe. David laid out the basic design for the terrace walls and paths. As time went on, Madeleine took the lead. Over the years the couple planted numerous trees, including stewartias, maples, oaks, ashes, and three redwoods. The understory included many species rhododendrons. They loved contrasts and delighted in bold ferns growing beside smaller, textured plants. Several strategically placed water pots still attest to Madeleine's deep delight in the play of tree-filtered light.

In Madeleine's cosmos, her garden was the place, an enclosure of passionate discovery to be shared. Here, then, is a modern book of hours opening to a more abundant life.

Madeleine's Sanctuary

a Foreword by David Streatfield

THE BRIEF ESSAYS IN THIS ANTHOLOGY were inspired in different ways by our garden, which Madeleine called "The Sanctuary."

After becoming a couple in 1982, Madeleine and I reluctantly became homeowners. A garden was not included in our original agreement. I should have been aware of the possibility.

Madeleine built estate gardens in Berkeley and Oakland in the 1970s, and brought tools and some favorite plants from California to Seattle. We were in our forties then and still vigorous. We purchased two lots on the upper west side of Queen Anne Hill in 1986. Our 1911 house sits on the northern lot, commanding memorable and unimpeded western and southwestern views of the city, Elliott Bay, and the Olympic Mountain range. From the street, the house appears to be a modest, two-story cottage; seen from the rear, due to a steep drop in topography, it is actually a towering, four-story structure.

Enclosed from the street by a high wood fence, the front garden possessed distinct Japonesque properties with a small standing rock, wooden decks, stands of bamboo, and cherry trees. Structure was provided by three tall trees close to the street, plus a massive Austrian pine and a handsome red maple tree. Below this relatively low area, the ground plunges steeply; it was dominated by an immense madrona beside the house amidst a riotous sea of blackberries and other noxious weeds, especially false bamboo. The glorious madrona was and remains the star of the garden, despite two major crown falls.

Eradication of the weeds required four to five years of very patient work. But our initial focus was the restoration of the poorly remodeled house. This was completed in early 1991. In 1992, a major windstorm knocked over three of the large trees in the front garden, heaving up portions of the sidewalk and destroying the entrance gate. This dramatic event provided the impetus for planning a new garden—a collaborative effort in which I assumed responsibility for the plan. Our collaboration, it struck us, somewhat resembled that of British diplomat Harold Nicholson and writer Vita Sackville-West at Sissinghurst Castle in England.

And my happy role evolved into being Yard Boy.

"The Sanctuary" is a woodland garden with an underlying geometry that served as Madeleine's canvas, on which she created art with plants. The front garden has a subtle, geometric structure with low walls that she built with blocks of broken concrete sidewalk. A grove of slender stewartia trees complements the remaining pine and red maple trees and defines a slightly depressed area we called the Gravel Pit, where we entertained.

Beneath the tree canopy, native ground covers are contrasted with a variety of boldly textured ferns and small rhododendrons and daphnes. During the summer months, carefully placed glazed pots are filled with water to enrich the garden with small flashes of sunlight and attract numerous birds for bathing and drinking. Outward views are hidden by a row of carefully pruned Callery pear trees.

On the steep slope, the madrona is partnered by a large California live oak, a gift from Madeleine's father. At the bottom of the garden, a Port Orford cedar, several small ash trees, a stand of tall redwoods, and a collection of the larger-leaved rhododendrons provide strong textural complexity. These trees and shrubs frame the beautiful southwestern view over Puget Sound.

The garden contains several microclimates. The steep hillside dominated by the madrona is run as a dry slope watered only by rain. Above and below the tree, extensive plantings of iris, species bulbs from Turkey, larger shrub roses, and peonies plunge down the sunny slope to the boundary.

Immediately below the house, a series of narrow terraces house several collections, including a small orchard of older apple species, a selection of old roses, pomegranates, lavenders, and vegetables. The terrace walls are draped in rosemary; three pruned pine trees punctuate the upper terrace. A beautiful, narrow, winding stone stair, contained by large clumps of clinker brick, links the front and lower gardens.

Changes were made in response to poor, initial decisions. The vegetable patch never worked in its original location; instead, we were able to grow vegetables successfully on the sunny deck at the rear of the house. Some plants were felled by severe frosts. Such changes occur in any garden.

But Madeleine's garden is distinguished by its meanings.

The garden played a central role in Madeleine's life. The Gravel Pit was a place for entertaining friends in the spring, summer, and early autumn. There are numerous personal associations. Madeleine's parents gave her several trees and shrubs. A large-leaved rhododendron and an old rose in the lower garden commemorate two beloved cats. The three pruned pine trees on the upper terrace served to remind us of the great stone pines of Rome, which we both loved.

But the meanings that clearly relate to her essays are bound up with the concept of sanctuary. Traditionally, sanctuaries are privileged places of comfort and reflection. Madeleine would often announce that she was "going to the garden." This was part of her deep search for meaning by being in the place she had fashioned. Here she contemplated the issues she wrote about. These ranged from philosophical musings to seemingly mundane garden management issues. Influenced by the Zen monks we had watched tending temple gardens in Japan, she realized that even the simple task of picking up leaves was not a tiresome, quotidian task, but potentially an important aesthetic act.

The enclosed upper and lower gardens provide physical protection from the outer world, but also afford subtle, long views toward the regional land and seascape. Such an aesthetically beautiful perch provided the basis for some of her deeper reflections on universal meanings, which included ruminations on the complete landscape, or universe, to be found within a single iris bloom.

Madeleine's poetic vision remains in her writings, and in the physical beauty of the sanctuary that inspired her.

Spring

The Japanese, of course, have a word for this—
hanagumori—*meaning blossom haze.*

Contemplative Time

HOW TEMPTING TO PLANT our bean seeds, bed out the new tender annuals, and prepare our big pots with their summer geranium displays.

We should think again.

March still carries the dangers of frosty nights, cold winds from the north, and cool, wet, sticky soil. The first hints of spring-like warmth have been visiting us these last few weeks and the buds are finally bursting from their shells, but that cold wind from the Arctic glaciers came last Sunday to remind us that the full and reliable warmth of spring is still just in our dreams.

However, there are good, robust chores to be done out in the garden, including the cleaning up of winter's debris and the edging of sodden lawns that have bled their winter wetness onto the surrounding hard surfaces.

This is also a very good time to clear the areas where you have plans for developing the new garden features, whether it is the new patio, the new perennial border, or finally the removal of sod to make way for new and exotic planting beds.

I

Get your measurements made so that you can calculate the materials needed. Why not beat the crowds to the garden supply shop?

On the really frightful, stormy days, pick one of our spring flowers and bring it to your table. Take the time to study it ever so closely, for these blooms are a world unto themselves, with markings and veining to delight the eye.

There it all begins.

March 1997

Bursting Spring

BRIGHT, CHERRY-PINK AND INTENSE, lemon-yellow have been the dominant colors in our local landscape these past two weeks. The huge splotches of color from the cherry trees and the forsythia bushes are matched by the low-lying bergenia blossoms and the big tufts of daffodils.

Daffodils have very few pests, and thrive without too much attention. Therefore, for the greatest splash of color, the 'King Alfred' daffodil has become the favorite. There is nothing mysterious or complex about this daffodil. The trumpet is as long as the surrounding perianth segments; there is one flower per stem, and the color is pure, strong yellow. They do well as a cut flower, and if you buy them by the fistful at your local flower merchant, you do not have to deal with the unsightliness of the yellowing foliage in your garden beds.

At the other end of the scale is the tazetta hybrid 'Tete-a-Tete'. Its leaves and flowers are just a delicate eight inches and the bloom, the size of your thumbnail, is a pure, slightly darker yellow. You often find these bedded out with primroses and grape hyacinths. These are perfect little daffodils for a planter box, elegant terrace pot, or out in the garden in an intimate setting such as a small rockery. The usual garden varmints—moles, gophers, slugs, snails, and raccoons—never bother with daffodil bulbs or blooms.

And then there are the all-time favorites, once you get past the obvious ones mentioned above. There's the *Narcissus* 'Actaea', commonly called the Poet's Daffodil. Its broad, white, overlapping perianth sections hold a tiny button of a trumpet, which is yellow with a touch of orange. Scattering these around your favorite, dark-maroon hellebore cultivars can significantly brighten up the area. I would keep them away from your snowdrop collections: when the Poet blooms, the snowdrops are just finishing, and their foliage is not attractive.

Narcissus x odorus 'Campernelle' makes lovely, delicate, but dense clumps of reed-thin foliage with pure yellow, slightly scented flowers. When you are out picking these blooms in the breezy breaks between rain squalls, you will think that there is just a single bloom for each stem. But when the indoor warmth hits them, usually another bloom opens just slightly below the first bloom. Their petals are curvaceous, architectural wonders, slightly curved back and twisting, while the small trumpet has the shape and character of a *Primula auricula* primrose bloom. With all their diminutive characteristics, these daffodils are tough warriors. I have never seen them battered down and messed up by a nasty March snow or bitter, cold event.

The over 2,000 named daffodils listed in the R.H.S. Plant Finder suggests that we have a wealth of choices for our gardens, and with the ease of the global and local searches, we can extend our knowledge and selections. Keep asking your local nursery for the "exotics"—that is, anything other than 'King Alfred,' and they will respond to your interests.

Ask them for *Narcissus bulbocodium*. This species is native to Spain, Portugal, and southwestern France. The flower buds seem to be just a light green, but when they open the very narrow petals become yellow and hold a bulbous trumpet. These delicate treasures have usually been available locally, but in very limited quantities. The common name is hoop-petticoat, and oftentimes they are seen combined with the *Fritillaria* bulbs.

The other species of daffodil that begs for our attention is *Narcissus cyclamineus*. For a long time, it was considered extinct or a figment of Pierre Vallet's imagination. However, it was rediscovered near Oporto, Portugal in 1885. With its swept-back perianth on top of the drooping trumpet, it is unique in its presentation. Again, a diminutive species, but worth the trouble for its sleek lines mixed in with moisture-loving ferns.

This daffodil does not tolerate dryness, and that is why we seldom see it available in the trade. The bulbs do not like long drying conditions. But if you were to present and pay for your order, it could probably be sent to you at the time the propagator was digging the crop.

Long live 'King Alfred' for its sheer exuberance, but I hope a door has been opened to investigate the extensive and exciting world of narcissus. Also, it was the Roman author, Pliny the Elder, who explained that narcissus got its name from the narcotic nature of its scent and not from the young boy Narcissus.

March 2006

Almost April

THE ASPARAGUS TIPS ARE PUSHING through the cold, damp soil. The maple trees are unfurling their leaves. The fuzzy, white sword fern fronds are straightening their backs and starting to show some tender green as they reach for the sky. The solitary crocus blooms that announced the new spring season have vanished, and the daffodils have done yeoman's duty this year by announcing the end of winter. Now the deciduous trees are filling our garden spaces with hazy, new growth, and today it looks as though the lilacs will soon be filling our gardens with their perfumed blooms.

We dream towards the early summer harvests: fresh salads, tender radishes, arugula for that peppery hit, and we long for the early raspberries and luscious strawberries. This is a time for extreme patience.

We are given a warm, soft, sunny day between the end-of-March gales, and despite any sort of internal wisdom, we move viscerally into warm, productive, summer-like days.

The seasons move fast. Maybe you have already prepared your productive garden plans, and the seeds and seedlings are just awaiting your installations in, of course, the perfectly prepared beds. Those beds are just bursting with fresh compost and are free of any invasive weeds. Any system of irrigation has been thoroughly checked out and "certified" efficient. All paths are clear of detritus. All the stakes that might be needed have been thoroughly cleaned, sanded, and are easily available, as they have been stacked in an orderly fashion.

Enough of this sort of dreaming. We are always a day late (or several), and yes, a dollar short.

As the season progresses, one of my favorite flowers has the ability to go easy on my occasional lapses into laziness. These are my nasturtium plants. Along with the California poppy seedlings, they both spring forth with great vigor every year. For me, these plants are very well-behaved. They never become invasive, and the ones I don't want (too close to my sacred *haricot vert* beans) can easily be weeded out. However, my first season here in Seattle, with the traditional nasturtiums, was a total disaster—they were covered with icky-sticky, black aphids early in August.

Since then I have learned about re-seeding those nasturtiums in late July, removing the almost-mature, but soon-to-be-aphid-infused, offending plants. Now I have great cascades of aphid-free, vigorous, and happy nasturtiums until mid-November. I let them romp through most of my lower, southwest facing garden. I love it when they clamber up into my sumac tree, throw themselves into and around the fading peony greens, and then march into, and climb, a great big shrub rose. Such wonderful insouciance at the end of our fall season.

Recently, our ever-persistent hybridizers have been bringing to market many exciting new variations of the traditional nasturtium. Not all of the newly available plants are the work of the hybridizers. The reason some of these plants are on the market is due to a renewed interest in this overlooked and common annual. An old-fashioned favorite of mine is 'Empress of India.' Its leaves are gray-green, and the plant mounds rather than vines. The deep, rose-red flower beautifully offsets the gray leaves, and I love to have the mounds interspersed with my lavender plants.

A recent favorite is the Alaska series, with its slightly mottled foliage and fragile orange, yellow, and red flowers. This nasturtium needs a special, secluded place; it looks washed-out and pathetic near the traditional, vigorously vibrant nasturtium.

Currently, the darkest nasturtium is called 'Black Velvet.' It sounds a bit thuggish, and plant enthusiasts who know their combinations suggest that the pale-yellow 'Milkmaid' variety be planted close by to soften the darkness.

Finally, of course, the hybridizers have produced a nasturtium, 'Margaret Long,' that does not produce viable seed, so that you can only include this plant in your garden by buying it as a fully developed plant at your nursery each year. However, it has amazing, double flowers of striped apricot colors.

Your friends will not believe that this is a nasturtium.

And a small footnote: nasturtiums are known as an edible plant—both its leaves and flowers.

March 2010

Sheer Nourishment

THE GURGLING OF THE DOWNSPOUTS was such a sweet sound early Saturday morning. With no perceptible wind noise, the spattering raindrops were like an almost-forgotten melody coming back to life. As I walked under a big umbrella, the raindrops drummed. Big ones, little ones, all very persistent. This was not a dramatic spring shower with great pyrotechnics such as thunder, lightning, glaring sun, and then dark, brooding clouds. Rather, it was a long, one-dimensional, gray day with the steady rain until just before sunset.

The tulips, by mid-afternoon, had lost their ability (or will) to remain upright, and laid themselves down onto the wet ground. The daffodils kept themselves more upright, but some were seen leaning a bit precariously by the end of the day. I suspect a strong breeze would have easily flattened them. The soil seemed to be expanding, just like a dry sponge finally fluffs after getting thoroughly soaked. Skinny worms were oozing across hard surfaces where small puddles stayed formed.

The wet air on my face, neck, and hair felt like a refreshing dip in a slightly cool lake. Breathing seemed easier as pollen and dust were washed from the air. It was a day meant for reading in bed, taking short walks, eating lightly, napping lightly, followed by more walks in the mild wetness. The brief, red-orange light at sunset was the sole color spot in the day's atmosphere. How could so much wet grayness feel so nourishing?

March 2005

Spring Blush

AT TIMES IT DOES FEEL THAT SPRING BURSTS forth with all her glories at once. Your eye is drawn to the vivid yellows of the forsythia bushes and the daffodils as they withstand the gusts of March. Suddenly Dravus Street and Florentia Street are lined with fully-blooming, purple plum trees. Meanwhile, there is also an amazing haze or almost undetectable film of color shimmering in the landscape from the slowly emerging deciduous trees and shrubs.

Looking closer, one is able to see the parts of this haze or film. It is the slow unfurling of the tightly wrapped new leaves or blooms. On the stewartia trees the tiny buds are pure white, dancing in the sun with glistening raindrops from the last shower. For a few days they get fatter, and then suddenly the trees are clothed in a tender, green shade. Their flowers will come later in the year in July.

As the catkins get longer each day on the birches and hazel trees, they create a tawny haze overall. The starkness of the bare winter branches becomes softened before their leaves unfurl. The fat buds on the lilac bushes and the magnolia trees give the plants a dark maroon presence, long before the blooms and the leaves appear.

This soft haze of growth is beginning to hide the old bird nests that have revealed themselves in the winter barrenness. We can surmise that new nests will be constructed when the leafy growth has again obscured our views.

Do we need the garish vitality of over-hybridized primroses to announce spring, or can we sharpen our eyes, stay quiet, stop the cell phone chatter, and truly see and feel spring blush as it rolls forward?

March 2004

Rethinking the Kitchen Garden

MAYBE THIS IS A GOOD TIME TO RETHINK the garden layout in relation to our homes and the way we live today. Traditionally, the kitchen garden was pragmatically placed near the servants' quarters, and was usually fenced to keep out marauding deer, rabbits, and other hungry vegans.

It was also seen as a working-class garden, with all the crops in neat rows for ease of mass harvesting. The productive crops were given a certain utilitarian respect in society, while ornamental plants were given pride of place, and were an indicator of our position in the community. Once, of course, certain lawns were designed to signal there was no need for productive crops at this particular address.

With the advent of the edible landscape design theory, it is now possible to think about the garden as a place to hold many kinds of plantings, some of which may feed us. In our urban gardens, most of us don't have room for a proper orchard, but we can certainly plant apple, pear, peach, and fig trees.

Maybe some of you have already done this and simply haven't put a design theory into practice.

It is the classic kitchen garden I like to think about. Do we really want to trek through the rain to bring in the early lettuces, gather the needed chives, cut a few sprigs of rosemary for the spring lamb dish, pull the young carrots, or get the first arugula leaves to brighten up the dinner salad?

Think about where you to and fro on a daily basis. We all have our beaten paths between our homes and our public lives. Wouldn't it be grand to pick up the lettuces along with the mail or the newspaper?

Aside from the ease of harvesting, we need to look at our productive crops with an eye toward their aesthetic beauty. A popular perennial is *Crambe cordifolia*, with its dramatic leaf form and spectacular, white burst of flower panicles. This plant is similar in form to the rhubarb; massed together they could make a striking display of foliage, flower, and edible plant within the ornamental garden.

The artichoke has a distinctive, blue-gray leaf and the promise of a beautifully articulated flower that can be cropped. Here in the Northwest, it needs to be considered an annual, but planted with other gray-leaved plants such as lavenders, ornamental sages, and lamb's ears, it can add a bold and beautiful essence within the gray border.

Basil plants can make an effective edging to any number of planting areas. I use the woodland strawberry, known in Europe as *fraise des bois*, as an edging plant in my deeply shaded rhododendron and fern garden. The thumb-size berries continue to appear as late as October, and each berry explodes with the essence of strawberry when eaten. These plants line my daily path to the outside world.

I eat them going out in the morning and when I return in the evening. Carrots produce a beautiful, feathery foliage and pale-white umbel flowers when allowed to keep growing. The tall foliage can add a dramatic, late-season height to the perennial border, and the tough old carrots can eventually be used in hearty autumn and winter soups and stews.

A friend of mine grows beautiful scarlet runner beans right beside his front door. Very few visitors can stop themselves from picking and eating one, or many, of the tender beans.

Finally, in a very formal garden estate, I once saw a zucchini plant being grown at the end of a verdant lawn, surrounded by rhododendrons, azaleas, and ferns. The first time I noticed the zucchini a strong shaft of sunlight illuminated its form. Each of its shiny leaves reached for the light. The soft, orange-yellow blooms caught the eye.

March 1996

Bad Weather and the Gift of Time

FROM THE SUBLIME TO THE RIDICULOUS becomes a perfect description for our Northwest spring season. Pelting hailstorms, bright splashes of sunshine, howling winds tearing at our exquisite cherry blossoms, and warm, sunny, late afternoons that are much too brief.

Yet, despite the frustrations of not being able to continue the excitement of the long working hours launched in the garden last week, these pauses in our outdoor schedules can be used quite judiciously for laying the groundwork for the successes ahead. All is not lost when garden time is cancelled on account of the weather.

Time has been given us to repair or buy tools. Gardening classes and demonstrations are much more rewarding when we know that nothing would have been achieved by staying home trying to work in the garden.

Additional seed packets can be found to fill in the annual flower border or the vegetable selection for this year. More time can be spent with books featuring great gardens, where we might find ideas for our own gardens.

In one book I happened upon a wonderful example of bergenia in bloom, and then a flowering cherry tree. Without an afternoon of rain, I wouldn't have found them.

March 1994

Spring Chill, and Then...

IN SPITE OF THE COOL TEMPERATURES, spring is rapidly unfurling its tender, new growth these days. I love this point in spring for all of its fragile tentativeness. The great bunches of bright, yellow daffodils catch our eye. The forsythia blooms remind us of that golden orb we so long to see, but which so often these days remains hidden behind gray clouds. And then the new cherry and plum blossoms show fortitude and beauty in the face of cold temperatures and occasional squalls.

These first spring offerings are not nestled amongst other vigorous growth; they are surrounded by the still, quiet barrenness of winter. We find in our deciduous trees the bird nests we did not see last summer. The trunks and branches are still dark with wetness. Four plum trees at the corner of Seventh West and West Crockett make you pause to admire their elegant structural beauty, now adorned with airy, white blossoms.

Looking down the side streets as you do your weekly walk through our communities, you can see soft, white, and barely pink hazes. The Japanese, of course, have a word for this—*hanagumori*—meaning blossom haze. You find your eyes searching for another haze effect, perhaps just over the ridge? But instead you find yourself stopped in your tracks by the mighty magnolia on West Highland Drive near Seventh West. The huge and strangely colored blooms are unlike the demure, fresh, popcorn-white blooms on other magnolias. And then there are the newly planted magnolias with yellow blooms, and of course the soft, pink, almost lilac-colored blooms of *Magnolia x soulangiana*. This renders an Easter-egg coloring to our landscapes.

When the sun is out, the overlooks in our neighborhoods are filled with photographers. I applaud their efforts and stand in awe at their ability to capture the beauty of our waters and snow-capped mountains. The air is crystalline clear. It draws us outside, away from our dark nesting holes of winter. The sun illuminates the rich and complex texture on the elongated trunks of the majestic madrona tree at the eastern end of the bridge on McGraw Street. The next day's walk takes you along the inaptly named Magnolia bluff to study those madrona groves. Regrettably, they continue to look in decline; however, one squints and hopes that the new growth will be stronger, now that protective fences have been installed.

Suddenly the day comes when that bare tree you pass every day shows a touch of green on its branches. What starts out looking so tentative is soon in full-flush. The barrenness of winter is rapidly disappearing.

What a delight to behold.

April 2009

Time to Finish

SEIZE THE MOMENT! is the gardener's battle cry for these wet, sometimes wild, spring days.

Due to the unpredictable weather, it's nearly impossible to create and observe a schedule for working in the garden. So, we can take a cue from the great gardeners: prioritize our routes, and break them into thirty-minute steps.

You'll be surprised at how much can be accomplished this way. For example: take the lawn edger tool out, and finish that routine, before unleashing the mower from the storage area. And finish the task at hand. That includes raking up the lawn-edge pieces and getting them into the yard waste bucket.

A word of caution: if you are trying to dethatch your lawn during this wet weather, wait for at least a twenty-four-hour dry spell before you do it. If water is still at or on the lawn's surface, the thatching tools will likely rip out the lawn along with the thatch. A twenty-four-hour wait is a good investment.

April 1993

Spring Ahead

ALL THOSE INCORRECT CLOCKS STARING at me the other morning made me want to pull the covers over my head! Tiny little buttons to push, and all needing a different sequence. Eh, *voilà*—victory, without resorting to reading any directions.

A few moments of smugness blissfully descended around my head. Then it was time to escape to the garden. Many new and wondrous shrubs were waiting to be planted.

For bare root plants, it is a good idea to soak the roots overnight. The planting instructions, for mail-ordered plants, just advise to plant as quickly as possible upon receipt. I have had many more successes with the overnight soaking method. Also, do not be afraid to prune back some of the roots to make the planting process easier. Believe me, the plant will thrive. The plant will not thrive, however, if it is planted too deep.

Getting the right height is the most challenging aspect for me. Laying the shovel across the planting hole, and measuring down, is great if you are planting on a level surface. But even then, after giving the plant a thorough soaking, there is always some slippage down. Pulling the plant straight up, and gently adding more (and by now mucky, wet) soil, eventually gets the plant at the right height.

The other planting challenge comes with those root-bound plants. Again, do not be afraid to cut the roots back, once you have wrestled them free from the pots. Any roots that are circling the plant in the pot will continue to grow in a circle once they are in the ground.

There are many diagrams available in books and leaflets about the proper planting techniques. For the novice gardener, it can seem overwhelming. For the seasoned gardener, they have, over the years, developed their own tricks and props to get the unwieldy beast planted upright.

Why is it that gardening shows and magazines make this spring planting season look so pleasant? It is brutally hard work in my garden. In the gardening shows, the soil always seems so fluffy. Just dig a hole, spread the roots out, backfill the hole, and water. Then spread some rich-looking mulch around, and sip a cool drink on the patio while you admire the perfect display of spring tulips.

Having a good, long soak in the tub, admiring the new bruises and torn nails, counting the number of shrubs planted and the number left to be planted this year, I got to wondering why all those digital timepieces didn't have an extra chip in them so they can reset themselves, just like my computer does twice a year?

April 2006

A Little Light Pruning

THE TENDER, NEW GROWTH is unfurling at a rapid clip these days.

By evening, the leaves seem twice the size as they were in the morning. Some of this new, exuberant growth is not where you want it to be; now is the prime time for light pruning.

The suckers appearing on the maples, crabapples, and other deciduous trees can easily be removed by just rubbing them off with your fingers. By removing this unwanted, new growth, you are directing the plants' energy straight towards the growth that you want to encourage.

For newly planted flowering shrubs, such as rhododendrons, it makes sense to remove some of the promised blooms so that the young plants will spend their energy on developing better roots and new leaves, rather than on the flowers this year.

When removing a rhododendron bud, try to simply twist it off rather than cutting it off—the new leaf buds are perilously close on the stem below the flower bud. And with all this luxuriant growth, our favorite weeds are rampantly growing also. Try to get to them before they set seed—a dream that we all have every year.

Thickly mulching the beds after weeding helps to discourage the coming crop of weeds, and it also helps to cover up all those that were just entirely too tedious to get out.

Actually, if truth be told, I like to weed, but only in small increments. I particularly like to weed during the first half-hour after I get home. It's a relaxing way to unwind and forget the noise of the day, and to greet again all the fresh new growth.

April 1996

Mulch: a Security Blanket

FROM CHERRY-SIZED HAIL to unseasonable warmth, the garden is moving ahead this season in strange and wonderful ways.

With the fullness of growth surrounding us, I still look on in amazement when I find a tree, such as the beech, just starting to leaf out. With the new warmth, my mind fast-forwards to summer's roses, but then I pull back. Thankfully, the cool days will return, giving us time to watch the slow unfolding of the rhododendrons and their showy colors.

However, when the gray, cool days return, it's time to watch for early dryness in our water-loving plant areas, and time to do the final weeding and mulching in our drought-loving planting areas. It's important to thoroughly weed those areas that will not receive irrigation in summer, and give them a good layer of mulch now, before the soil dries any further.

Think of the mulch as a security blanket for your plants. It keeps the soil protected from the harsh rays of the sun, and provides an insulating layer that keeps the soil in a perfect, friable condition.

This soil condition promotes deep root growth, and good utilization of the water in the soil from past winter rains. The spring bulbs may also need to be deadheaded as they finish this year's bloom.

Think about some annual seeds to plant in your spring bulb areas: love-in-a-mist, cosmos, and nasturtiums are excellent choices.

April 1995

Words of Wisdom from 1894

OVERWHELMED AND MADE NEARLY speechless by the splendors and forcefulness of the season, I will, this week, defer to another's writing. I think you'll understand why.

But it is neither wise, nor tender, nor loving, to remit to others, however expert, the supreme care of one's garden. You will tend yours with your own hands and discover its needs with your own heart; and if, in doing so, you have to withdraw yourselves sometimes, more than accords with modern wont, into rural seclusion, your social instincts will not therefore be starved, nor your share in the graces and charities of life thereby be curtailed.

You will find much resemblance between flowers and human beings; for they too grow reserved under coldness or maltreatment, and respond with almost feminine alacrity to every sympathetic endeavor to apprehend them.

The quotation is from the dedication written by Alfred Austin to Madeleine & Dorothy Stanley in the first edition of his book, *The Garden That I Love*, published in 1894.

While I can pause and ponder on his thoughts regarding "feminine alacrity," I prefer to be inspired by his preceding words. The personal discovery and needs of the garden can be met through the actual, tactile work of the garden in spite of the sense of social detachment.

There will be time soon enough to turn back towards society.

April 1994

Sword Fern: a Primeval Unfolding

THE GARDEN CONTINUES to come to life. The spring bulbs are in full glory, beneath deciduous trees filled with tender, new leaves.

There is a sense of a grand unfolding, and nothing represents this better than the sword fern crosiers that are lifting their heads skyward. These new fern leaves are often also called fiddleheads, and are the edible part of the fern plant. Each day brings greater emergence as the crosiers unfurl in scroll-like fashion. There is no riotous color to attract the eye, so why the intense fascination? For me, they evoke a sense of the primeval, the unfolding, the unbending, the loosening of a beginning.

We are so fortunate to have a tough, hardy native— the sword fern. It's so common we almost dismiss it here, yet it is a highly prized fern in other parts of the country. Ferns have not been hybridized for the home garden, so having a fern collection in your garden brings a touch of wild nature to your garden. Surprisingly, they are remarkably tough plants, and will thrive through adaptation to ordinary garden soils.

April 1995

Behold the Grape Hyacinth

IT IS A MYSTERY TO ME that the wonderful, yet modest, grape hyacinth, *Muscari armeniacum*, is not used more often as part of our spring-flowering bulb displays.

I find this lovely plant in older gardens, but hardly at all in newer plantings. A shame. It's inexpensive, reliable, and naturalizes very well. Its matte-blue color is a rare treat among all the pinks and yellows of the season.

I have planted these bulbs with deep purple pansies growing through their grass-like foliage, and I always add just five or six small red species tulips, such as *Tulipa hoogiana*.

The glaucous foliage of the tulips, and their height, give the needed accent to the massing of the hyacinths.

Next year, I plan to start naturalizing the grape hyacinth bulbs with some of my deciduous ferns; their fronds are unfurling now, and I think that they will form a good cover for the bulbs' withering foliage.

April 1994

Thugs in Spring

POW! SPRING HAS EXPLODED.

With the warm winter, and then the drenching rains, luxuriant growth is rampant. It did seem to slow a bit with last week's nippy temperatures, but not for our stalwart weeds. The brilliant dandelions appear to double in numbers and showiness every hour. The chickweed mats ooze across the terrain, while that perky pest, named shotweed, seems to be in fast-forward on its second go-round. For some dedicated gardeners, the tender growth tips of the chickweed and the leaves of their dandelions end up in their salad bowls. I applaud their approach, but thankfully, I do not seem to have enough dandelions to fill my salad bowl.

The real pests for me in the garden are sweet, blue-flowering, profuse seeders. Let's start with borage. It is very easy to grow from seed. While it flops over and should probably be staked in a tidy-garden atmosphere, the heavenly blue flowers add a spicy touch to summer salads, and seem to bring the blue skies down to the garden. Also, it grows quite well with or without water. It's a great plant, until the following year, when the seedlings are everywhere; cute little flat things, hiding under the mulch, around the base of plants, in walls, in paths, and not too easy to pull out. With due diligence, the darlings seem to have been eradicated, until the second year when there is a plethora of seedlings again in all the usual places.

The second is the forget-me-not. Another exquisite blue flower, so charming and innocent until they go to seed, and create mats of seedlings which need to be lifted with a pitchfork. How can this diminutive plant behave so badly?

So, while we revel in the beauty of springtime, the supremely fast-paced growth surrounding us brings great guilt, along with pleasure. Suddenly, we have to go into overdrive, and grab those moments of intense sunshine between hailstorms to tackle our nemesis plants. All dedicated gardeners have their special choice of vigorous thugs to conquer. The ridiculous absurdity is that each year we think we can control all this extravagantly beautiful spring growth.

I try to stay amused.

April 2005

Noise and Silence

SLIPPING INTO THE WARMTH of my bath, I hear out the window the screech of wheels, the noise of a train along the Elliott Avenue corridor below the Hill, and the repetitive sound of the wheels turning, the familiar train rhythm, and then the thin wail of its horn.

Thoughts run astray. Open land where the horizon dwindles into endlessness. The wonder of where the train is going: what lies in those lands? The drawn-out sound goes on, making me realize that this is a long train. How will motorists react while they wait, and then wait even longer at a railroad crossing? I wait to hear the end of the noise, expecting it to soon cease, but it goes on.

Finally, I can hear a gull calling. And the far-off sound of the train is still there. I shift in my bath, and I wonder. The terribly evocative sound of the train conjures up such a rich tapestry of feelings, of memories in our lives. For Americans, it is the idea of new beginnings in some other place. For Europeans, it is the connection between different cultures.

A car goes by on the street outside. After it passes, there is still the faint sound of the train. Now more gulls can be heard screeching in the night air. I wait for the last of the train noise, expecting a contemplative silence. The train is well on its way, but the silence is not there. Instead, I can hear the noise of airplanes overhead.

Perhaps the silence will come after they're nearer their landings. But after their noise ends, a steady stream of white noise from the passing cars on a main street several blocks away appears. The train is gone, having briefly interrupted the persistent hum of the city. Without that interruption, no notice is given to the quiet, evening noise of our urban life.

April 2004

Finally, the Buds are Popping

THERE IS THIS AMAZING chartreuse haze in our landscapes. The dark background setting of our firs and
cedars only enhances this slightly acrid haze. Yes, it
is our bigleaf maples, and the new flowers on our
madrona trees, and all the budding new growth that
holds this ephemeral lightness, including the soft
redness seen in the unfurling plum and red maple
trees. The skies have been scudding with spring grayness, intermixed with brilliant moments of intense
sunlight. I am not sure that the most brilliant stage
designer could produce such a dramatic and hope-in-
spiring landscape.

This unfurling from the tightness of the winter
landscape moves at an incredibly fast pace. On warm
days, you can almost hear the new growth. Then the
gray descends again, but if you can see past your own
disappointment, those buds are still fattening, and
reaching out and up for the light.

Our native sword fern is a joy to watch unfurl.
Yet, it is not often used, much less celebrated, in our
home gardens. I suspect that is because, out in our
more untended parts of the garden, it is just a soggy
pile of dark green and brown fronds. Within a garden
it can hold its own on several fronts.

Except for cutting back the old fronds in March,
it is maintenance-free. It is drought-tolerant, except
for an intense western exposure. Yes, it can survive

in soft sunshine. Look at its native range, and you see that it is a superior erosion-control plant. But until you bring it into your personal garden, its fine properties remain elusive.

I combine my sword ferns with an amusing collection of *Dryopteris* cultivars. Find the ones that intrigue you. They also require nothing more than removing the old fronds, so that you can clearly see, and be thrilled by their unfurling fronds, which are not as hairy and tawny as the early fronds of the sword fern. Rather, they tend to be a raspberry or tawny pink to deep burgundy. Mix in a few early crocus and snowdrop bulbs, and some small species *Epimediums*, and your almost maintenance-free spring garden can give such a wonderful sense of enchantment as we wait, and wait, and wait...for the soft allure of summer.

April 2013

Shinryoku

JUST ENOUGH RAIN HAS FALLEN to make a baseball game a muddy affair, and to keep the slugs actively sliming their way through our garden treasures. Yet it is not enough rain to penetrate the new, unfurling canopies of our deciduous trees.

Check under your evergreen trees and shrubs, and you will find dry soil conditions. Check under and around other plants, and you will find that the soil is scarcely as muddy or sodden as it was just a few short weeks ago. This sudden dryness is in such contrast to the tender, verdant growth that is happening with such abandon throughout our landscapes.

Spring in the Northwest is a watery affair. The days usually start with a wet, deep grayness, and then come to a stunning end as slanting rays of sunshine light up the glistening drops remaining from the morning wetness. There may be the drama of a sudden, and slightly violent squall, with the wind tearing at the tender, new growth. But as a dear, bright, articulate gardening friend said recently, the faster the wind blows, the faster the squall is over.

With the lingering sunshine in the evening hours, we dream of the months ahead filled with hiking our favorite trails, sailing into new harbors, picnics with friends, and warming our bodies and souls with the full and warm summer light. But I am sorry to remind all of us that we have yet to reach "boating" opening day, the first Saturday in May (always miserably cold and wet), or the Fourth of July, also predictably wet and cool here in the Northwest.

So, we need to find ways to treasure those moments of dramatic squalls, the tender new growth, and the sense of renewal that surrounds us every day. The Japanese have a word, or rather a *kanji*, for this season—*Shinryoku*, which briefly translated means "new green." It also directly refers to the fresh verdure of spring.

Last year I was fortunate to be in Japan for their *Shinryoku* season, which lasts from the end of April through the first week in May. People travel to their favorite sights to view the new green. As you travel through their islands by train, you can see this chartreuse verdure in the hillsides. Their rice paddies show just a very modest, green glint. It is a time to renew, and they take that time to create an awareness of the season. For years I have been grappling with finding the words, or a word, that could capture the intensity and the simplicity of this time of the year. I found it: *Shinryoku*.

April 2007

Swiftly Fly the Days

IT FEELS AS THOUGH IT WAS just a mere three weeks ago that we all noticed the first crocuses of the year blooming.

And wasn't it just last week that the daffodils were in full force, and the tulips just getting ready to put on their dramatic show?

This spring season has been in a full and glorious sprint mode, and many of my friends and acquaintances have remarked on its exquisite, and mostly refined, beauty this year. But the signs of the summer garden are beginning to show.

First, we all have little, or in some cases, not so little, clusters of treasured plants that we brought home from all the spring plant sales, and they have yet to be planted out into our gardens. Some of us are still trying to clean up the vegetable garden areas. Yes, that should have been done at least by the end of February, but somehow life intervened with her demands.

The peonies are starting to burst with their three week, over-the-top displays. They make such wonderful cut flower arrangements. The vegetable beds stay abandoned as I rush a fistful of just-opening peonies to a local nursing home. Yes, there is something so much more powerful in homegrown, rather than store-bought bouquets. But we must thank and support our local merchants for providing us with cut flowers through all seasons. Perhaps it adds to the carbon footprint of our lives, but that vase of tulips, glowing on the table in the weak winter light of late January, refreshes the soul.

Watching the blooms on the crabapple and apple trees, I wonder whether there will be enough bees around to do the pollinating work this year. The implications from the current bee loss are so overwhelming that I think the story is being significantly played down. It is almost inconceivable to realize that we could suddenly not have pollinators for our crops. That is just too large an idea to work with. Surely those that know will find the reason for the loss, and swiftly supply the cure. But what if ...

Absolutely too scary to contemplate. I go out to find and name the roses that are starting to bloom in my garden. Roses and peonies and derelict vegetable beds—this is the type of garden that one never sees in the glossy garden books or magazines. But it is a garden that provides a soothing retreat from the cacophony and madness, slings and arrows, of life.

April 2007

A Beautiful Rock Wall

ROCK WALLS CAN SUPPORT more than Snow-in-Summer or Basket of Gold.

These plants seem so charming when first viewed, for they bloom profusely. But then they turn into garden thieves, crowding out most of our other planting experiments on, above, or below the wall.

The greatest proponent of rock wall planting was Gertrude Jekyll, British horticulturist, garden designer, and writer. She encouraged the use of seeds, and pointed out that most garden plants that do well in the flower border do just as well and sometimes better in a wall.

I saw a beautiful, blue columbine in a wall the other day—it was stunning.

Foxgloves and mullein, which readily come from seed, can add dramatic vertical elements at the right point in a wall. A *Rosa wichuraiana* will scramble happily over a wall, trailing its floppy branches down and around the stones.

This white rose blooms all summer, followed by attractive, orange-red hips in the autumn. It's important to get past the small plant syndrome, like the creeping thymes, unless, of course, your wall is just one to two feet high.

For larger walls, go boldly into experimenting and stop the dull wall thugs like *Cotoneaster horizontalis* from being your only wall plant choice.

If the rocks are dark in color, lighten the whole space by using gray-green plants such as santolina, with an additional thrust of blue from the cascading rosemary.

May 1996

Mind the Rhodies

THERE HAS BEEN A MAGNIFICENT display of rhododendron blooms this year in our gardens. I believe this richly colored fullness is a direct response by the plant to last year's drought.

Therefore, it becomes imperative that these blooms not be allowed to set seed, for this will further sap the plant's energy. If you spend just twenty minutes a day, preferably in the cool of the evening, the deadheading chore will soon be accomplished. Additionally, by starting immediately, you'll have the pleasure of seeing the tender new growth emerge, and you will gain an appreciation of the plant and its form and texture in your landscape. With thoughtful pruning and shaping, the rhododendron becomes a fine plant to admire in all seasons, with its flowers being only one aspect of its overall grandeur.

On another note, those late afternoon windstorms last week raised havoc in our gardens. I went out to pick the first branch of my favorite shrub rose, only to find a collection of stamens where the blooms had been.

Check out and clean up all your corners and crevices where the wind blew the debris. Also, look under any large-leaved or closely growing plants. If the debris is left in place, it will promote a lovely new home for slugs and other plant-chewing critters.

This is the time to check all staking and tying you had done in preparation for the season, and prune back any wind-damaged branches or flower stalks.

May 1997

Drought

YES, IT IS HERE IN THE MARITIME, rain-drenched Northwest.

You may still want to disbelieve, but we are dry, and the prospects for avoiding drought conditions do not bode well again this year. This has been a sneaky drought. It was five years ago that it settled in, making its existence hard to deny. In my bones, and watching my beloved trees and shrubs, the plants have been telling me loud and clear.

I was surprised earlier this year to hear from the state's respected climatologist that all was well. It did not feel that way to me, even with the incessant rains that started early in October of last year. Yes, it rained in October, drizzled in November, froze in December, and rained again a bit in January, but since then we have had open and mild weather. Yes, these balmy days have been thoroughly enjoyable. I love not being bundled up in rain gear.

But the earth is parched here in the western United States. News of the early wildfires in southern California should be read as a clear sign of severe drought. West of the Cascades, we are a part of that climate pattern.

The rainfall this past weekend was certainly a welcome relief, but it will do little towards changing the drought conditions. With our deciduous trees in full leaf now, very little water can penetrate the soil below their canopies.

So, why wait for the rules to be laid down? Let your lawn go brown, and start to think about all the ways you can better use this precious resource called water that we all take for granted.

May 2004

Planting the Crops

WHILE PREPARING AND PLANTING this year's vegetable beds, I was struck by the contrast between the full, vigorously blooming garden beds that surround the stark, but neatly made, vegetable beds. Such enthusiastic chaos meets tidiness. Or does the plain openness of the vegetable beds create a calm clearing in the exuberant garden jungle at this time of the year?

We are all taught to plant our vegetables in neat rows to maximize the exposure to sunlight. And then, the proper thinning of the seedlings will commence in a few days or weeks. I always find the thinning part to be quite troublesome, for I seem to pull up all the seedlings' neighbors, and so I leave two or three side-by-side to tough it out for themselves.

While preparing the beds, I try to take out the many pebbles and rocks that have moved to the surface. I could go and fetch the beautiful sieve that my father used for sifting the soil in his pristine and productive vegetable gardens, but I choose not to take the time. I suspect that I believe that no matter what attention to detail I pursue, my vegetable gardening will never match his perfection.

And I am in awe of those neat rows of tasty lettuces that people are able to create in their productive gardens. Have you ever seen the size of lettuce seed? It is miniscule! And carrots? How can that tiny seed produce those gorgeous, orange vegetables?

I have to go with the surefire, big seeds. I love the French *haricots vert* (green beans). So tasty and tender, and when they start producing, you can eat the beans for breakfast, lunch, and dinner every day. Saturating yourself with green beans for six to eight weeks makes it possible to never have to buy those tired, limp, and tasteless string beans sold at the supermarkets. The bushes stay small and never need staking. Lemon cucumber is another favorite, and again, an easy-to-manage small bush and prolific crop.

Mix in some of the wonderful varieties of sunflowers, arugula, and radishes for your salads, edge it all with trailing nasturtiums, and the vegetable beds look productive and tasty. It always amazes me that pushing these seeds into the freshly tilled soil will create, in such a short time, delicious treasures from my own garden for my meals. It also greatly deepens my appreciation for our local farmers and their beautiful produce at our farmers markets.

May 2003

Let Us Now Praise the Brown Lawn

ON THE STREET AND IN THE MEDIA, there's talk about our unseasonably warm spring following our mild, dry winter.

Even without all the talk, I would already know something was amiss, for my usual dense colonies of aphids adorning my shrub roses in May have turned up missing this year, much to my pleasurable astonishment.

However, my rhododendrons started to look very tired, shortly after their new growth unfurled—just as certain other young shrubs started to droop. I am pleased to report that they all responded very well after a twenty-minute irrigation effort on my part.

We all know that our lawns will soon require an inch of water every week, so the decision now is when to let them go brown. Brown lawns can look very handsome if they are cared for as meticulously as their green cousins. They need to be edged, thoroughly weeded, and raked clean of debris.

By creating and carefully maintaining a brown lawn, the water saved can be applied to our garden plants. The rhododendrons and camellias will be healthier this year if their spent flowers are removed immediately after the fullness of their bloom.

The plants will then have spent no energy on the setting of seed, and their new growth will come earlier and be heartier. This also holds true for annuals, perennials, and other small shrubs.

Perhaps it is my laziness, or maybe an inner voice whispering, "I have to mow the yard again tonight," that causes me to see a handsome beauty in a well-maintained, dormant lawn.

If so—good.

May 1994

A View of September from May

THE GARDEN IS SO FULL of visual delights on these warm, long days. The irises have sent their standards high into the light, while the roses begin to offer their beauty to the beholding eye.

The peonies have sneaked their gorgeous blooms into our hearts and minds these past days, while the coral bells sent up their wands to wave in the winds that arrive to clear the air. The vegetable gardens are beginning to fill out with their promise of abundant harvest, and the herb gardens are beginning to produce their promised flavors.

Working with coriander, and getting this season's basil plants established, reminded me of the tastes of summer while the lettuce gives us our first, fresh salads.

It all happens so fast, once the warmth and light have arisen.

If you, like many others, are just now trying to start a garden—take heart—and plant your zucchini and other squashes, including the pumpkin. Plant sunflower and nasturtium seeds, arugula, and radish seeds. All of these plants will grow, and fill your bare spaces with wonderful, edible plants this year.

Take garden tours, and take many notes and pictures. Go to the nurseries and look with awe at their fine displays. Then, flip your calendar to the third week in September, and mark it with a big note, reminding you that *this* is the time to start planning next year's garden.

September through the beginning of spring is the time to remove the weed-filled sod, the time to install irrigation systems, and the time to prepare the land for the rush of summer bounty.

The dedicated gardener must be able to see through the days and months ahead.

May 1995

White Skies

YES, WE ALL STOPPED in our tracks as the temperatures soared into the eighties—and the skies lost their
azure tones. White skies hovered as the heat lingered.
Mountain ranges were hazed into oblivion.

Such scurrying to get the grill clean. The same
goes for getting the tables, chairs, and pillows ar-
ranged again on the decks and patios. Unwinding the
tight, winter-cold, kinky hoses reminded us again
just how tiresome it can be to drag them around the
summer garden.

Yet, how fine to sit outdoors, offering your friends
this year's first official gin and tonic, and watch the
late afternoon light filtering through our landscapes.
I noticed that the light slanted differently than the
summer light. Hmmm ... I need to study where we are
with the arc of the sun in mid-May, as opposed to early
August or mid-September.

Despite the fantastic excitement of such unexpected warmth, the truth has always been that as of mid-
May, our soils start to dry out and close up. Even when
the marine air still imposes gray skies and drizzle, the
drying of our soils has started in a big way. The native

soil is gravelly till, left by the glaciers that scraped (and I might add, formed) the Puget Sound landscape.

The native soil forms a concrete-like density when it dries. Even if you have brought in expensive and "rich" soil, the drying effect is still happening. Think for a moment: if this drying effect were not happening, we would be living in a lush, jungle-like environment, with everything around us soggy, the ambient air filled with humidity.

So many gardeners believe we live in the same environment as England. May I suggest that you follow our latitude around the globe? You will find that we live in the same latitude as southern France. Of course, this brings to mind fields of lavender, olive trees, and vineyards.

In order to keep our rhododendrons, ferns, maple trees, coral bells, lilies, daphnes, and all our other beloved native and Asian native plants happy in this dry, Mediterranean climate, we must mulch heavily, and irrigate with wisdom. I have never believed in soaker hoses, because those shiny, black earwigs love the shelter of the tiny holes. They soon clog the outlets while you are busy tending to other challenges in your garden. Too soon, you become painfully aware that a plant is suffering from drought.

I prefer to spend a quiet time in the last light of day gently watering my garden with a handheld sprinkler. The peace and quiet, with bird song keeping me gently focused away from all the noise of the day, brings such pleasure.

The severe drying effect on our soils in this region creates a situation that replicates your kitchen sponge. With a bone-dry sponge placed under the spigot, water dances right off the surface, splashing all around. It takes a bit of maneuvering to get the sponge to function as one would expect. By spending the time gently spreading some water around your garden in the evening, you are opening the dry soil.

In the early morning, it is time to set the sprinklers on the garden beds. I suggest that each station should have at least twenty minutes of "water application." With deep soakings such as these, they only need to be done every five to seven days, unless you find a dry spot. Then when the rains return in the autumn, you are through with watering. And there will be no "irrigation" system failures!

The vegetable and fruit gardens will consume our time and talents for the next two months as we seed, transplant starts, and nurture our productive areas. Whew, good thing we had a taste of warmth recently. It renewed our courage for the stamina we will need to fully embrace our expectations for summer and fall.

May 1995

The Magic of Water Islands

WHAT WITH THESE RECENT WARM temperatures and the spring growth, who doesn't dream about having what is called these days a "water feature" in their garden?

However, does the thought of marauding raccoons, or the trouble with an appropriate electrical outlet, or the concern of visiting children and their safety, detract from the idea of a "pond" or "waterfall" in your garden?

Then think about the beauty of a single sheet of water, glistening and reflecting the colors of the sky on a still day. These flat-water surfaces also illuminate the patterns of raindrops and ripple with the wind. They also provide a place for the birds to take a drink and a break from their nesting activities—much like the old-fashioned water coolers at work where we gathered to tell stories.

We are fortunate to have many local garden stores now offering pots without holes in their bottoms. These pots can be in the form of water jars or shallow bowls or urns of differing sizes. The key to making these intriguing, without the fuss of water plants or cascading water, is to have the water absolutely level.

This takes a bit of doing, but once the shims are in place and the water is floating level to the eye, the magic begins.

I have come to believe that these "water islands" add an integral element to our Northwest gardens. They speak to our geographic position of looking west towards the Pacific and the Far East, with their concept of contemplative simplicity.

May 1997

Mulch and…Mulch

OUR LONG STRETCH OF WARM weather has a garden growing at a much faster rate this year. It's important to check your vine supports now, and ensure that the new growth is well-supported, but not strangling.

The rhododendrons need to have their spent blooms removed. They also need to receive an application of fertilizer and deep watering, for this is the time when their new growth, and the setting of their buds for next year's blooms, occurs.

Check your fruit trees, and thin the crop if it is heavyset. Start planting gladioli at two-week intervals for a succession of blooms later this summer. Finish the last of the spring bulb cleanup and weeding, and then mulch, mulch, mulch the garden beds.

Talk with your neighbors and see if you can't all get together and order a four- cubic-yard delivery of mulch. It's wonderful to have a grand supply of this material, which can be stored very nicely in yard waste bags or in unused garbage cans.

Once you have a liberal supply of mulch, you might wonder how you ever gardened without it. By keeping the garden beds thickly covered, the plants need less watering, and the weeding chores seem to evaporate. Mixing your garden soil with the mulch, you can make your own fine potting soil for those containers you create for your annual display of color.

I would not, however, recommend that you use this mix for the containers you use year-round. That requires a better quality, more pot-culture-specific, soil.

May 1995

Trees: Think Small

SO OFTEN, WHEN WE GO to specialty nurseries, we find ourselves focused on roses, or berries, or peonies. The list could maybe be expanded to include herbs, vegetables, and rare and exotic perennials.

What we so often overlook are the small trees.

At the big nurseries and garden centers, the tree offerings usually come in the eight to twenty foot variety, with corresponding price tags. And then we ponder—how to get them home, and into the ground— even if we've decided the hefty price is justifiable.

Once home, planted and staked, they become focal points. And, as far as focal points go, these new acquisitions can disappoint. They command our focus, and yet they seem so alone and skinny. A strident voice calls out that perfection is on the way. After all, we all want an instant effect, an instant tree.

Instead, I suggest starting with a small pup—say, a two to five-foot tree. The price will please you. Surround the new tree, or trees, with billowing annuals and perennials; the tree will be much happier nestled among plants—rather than standing as a lonely sentinel.

Should the tree ever fail to thrive due to wrong location or neglect, the other plants will fill in the empty space without blinking. By the third year the young trees will have grown their roots deep into the soil and—POW!—their vigorous growth will have your back against the wall. Wonderful, healthy trees will emerge from within the planting beds; within five years their growth will have surpassed the big, expensive trees.

As English writer and garden designer Mirabel Osler put it: "This sense of a tree's intransigence is a mainstay in a world treated as expendable."

May 1997

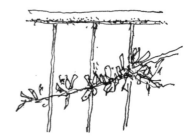

Take a Seat in the Sun

HELLOOOO SUN!

While we've been waiting for this glorious end to the incessant rains of late, the plants have been happily filling out with lush, and full, new growth.

While clearing out the jungle-like effect, I am always amazed to see how some of the weeds camouflage themselves with nearby plants. Several times I stepped past a group of foxgloves, admiring their tall spires, and completely overlooked the giant and succulent dandelion-like weed standing tall and proud among the foxglove spires. Or, I miss the invasive bindweed contentedly nestled at the base of a thorny rose bush, quietly sending up tough, new, choking growth hidden from the eyes admiring the first rose of summer.

It can feel completely overwhelming and oppressive looking at all there is to be done in the garden, now that the full light of summer illuminates its grandeur.

Even those of us who garden year-round can't keep pace with the season's prolific growth, let alone get all those new plants into the ground.

So, take the time to sit and feel the sun. Have a basket, a trowel, and a pair of pruners close at hand. Wander about aimlessly, look at the emerging flowers, cut back any interfering, rampant growth, pull a few weeds, and tidy up the last of the spring bulb foliage.

Soak up more sun and revel in the fact that all this glorious new growth is effectively covering up multiple minor sins and omissions.

May 1996

Summer Day and a Half

THE RETURN OF OUR BEAUTIFUL Northwest evenings allows us to once again begin our after-dinner strolls around the neighborhood.

We can enjoy and learn from our neighbor's gardens—both their successes and failures. An innovative staking solution—or unusual plant combination—usually unleashes some imaginative solution for my garden. If a garden's creator is out working in the evening hours, a conversation will often flow on at an agreeable length. As the light wanes, problems and solutions are shared. I have often returned home with my arms full of treasures, which might include the season's first head of lettuce, herb cuttings, rose cuttings, or some extra iris tubers.

It has been my experience that those who love to garden possess a compelling need to share their knowledge, whether it involves pest control, dahlia tubers, or the latest success from the worm composting front.

It's also possible to learn from the mistakes of others. Is there a garden bed that leaves you feeling confused—until you realize that your sense of discomfort has been caused by the owner's use of too many plant types? It helps to see the great gardens, and also those that just might be suffering from the same issues as yours. They tell us that not all is lost, and they give us ideas to bring home to the garden—with new eyes, too.

May 1994

Sharing the Knowledge

SUDDENLY, LAST FRIDAY, summer-in-spring arrived. There was not a lot of fanfare. The day just started with the standard chill to the air, but by noon, the air had a newfound warmth. The edgy chill was gone. And the forecast called for even warmer temperatures through the weekend.

Other cities have their own great "party" days, such as Pasadena with its Rose Bowl Parade or New York City's Thanksgiving Day Parade. Seattle's party day happens with that first warm, summer-in-spring day. Suddenly it seems as though everyone owns a convertible and wears sunglasses and short-shorts. The streets and sidewalks are brimming with a festive sense of total abandonment.

The only jarring note throughout the weekend was the incessant noise of the "lawn care" machines. I know that there is no simple solution to this type of noise pollution. And grinding my teeth and cursing softly does nothing to further the chances of finding a solution. I know that it makes better sense to stay with the great party feeling, and savor each fleeting hour of the bright and soft warmth.

Sure enough, the rains returned early Monday morning. But not the chill—and once again a warming trend will build all week, resulting in another perfect summer-like weekend.

However, I would be remiss if I did not add a note of caution. From now on, these gentle rains will do little to irrigate our gardens. The deciduous trees are now fully leafed, and while they provide a welcome, shady canopy later in the summer, right now they provide a canopy that blocks the rain. You will need to start irrigating any non-drought-tolerant plant under this canopy.

Regarding the art of irrigation, it cannot be said often enough—water is a scarce resource, and we must use it wisely. Water early in the morning or after sundown. Do not water for a mere ten minutes. That will bring all the roots to the surface, and then when a true heat wave hits, the plants will suffer greatly. Or die.

Except for the vegetable beds, a long deep soaking once a week can suffice for the rest of the growing season. And, of course, we are all proud of our late summer, brown lawns. They have become an iconic symbol of proper water usage.

May 2010

The Long-Awaited Arrival

HOPE YOU WEREN'T OUT OF TOWN on May 14, because we had a summer-in-spring day that broke all the records.

It just kept getting warmer and warmer and warmer. The sidewalks soon filled with late afternoon strollers and the roads with cyclists. The next day, we all set out to enjoy another beautiful warm day, but by mid-day the marine air had rushed back into town. It was cold, very cold by sundown! Since then, nothing but gray skies with some sun breaks, lots of squally wind, just enough rain to make the slugs happy, and then the amazing downpour Sunday afternoon. And the experts caution us that it is still too early to plant tomatoes!

Why did I think this year would be smooth sailing in the vegetable patch? A total memory loss has occurred about the vagaries of May weather. I thought I was so late seeding out the squashes and beans, sunflowers and cucumbers. They haven't popped yet, and I think I now know why—the soil temperature is still too low, while the rest of the garden is in such full glory. The peonies are flowering profusely, and they make such good cut flowers. Their blooming season lasts for just three or four weeks, but what a fine garden plant. Given full, sunny exposure, they can thrive without much irrigation; they just need their seed pods removed after flowering. And in late autumn, remove their dried foliage. My idea of a well-behaved plant. I find myself planting more of them each year.

All the different irises are in full bloom. It is good to see more gardens, including *Iris douglasiana* varieties. I think they provide a gentle contrast to the sturdiness and overblown blooms of the German iris. Also, *Iris graminea* has made a return. A few years ago, it was almost impossible to find this treasure, but thanks to the internet, growers have started to stock it, due to the number of requests. I believe this iris fell out of favor because of its modest blooms nestled within the leaf blades. But once you breathe its plum-like scent and observe the markings on its bloom, you know that it is a must-have treasure for your garden.

Then there are the early roses, the hedgerows of divinely-blue *Ceanothus*, and the purple sparklers on the Spanish lavender—our gardens are running amok, even without the warmth of summer days.

May 2007

In Praise of the Folly

THE RENEWED INTEREST in gravel paths and terraces has spawned innumerable articles on how to create these features and to keep them free of invasive weeds.

I go ballistic each time I read the advice from the experts—they are creating entirely too much work.

The advice usually includes some sort of weed-barrier cloth to be laid down after applying generous applications of weed-killing potions to the area to be graveled.

The depth of gravel is recommended to be two inches.

Please, please, please dig out the path or terrace space to a depth of four to six inches; forget the poisons and the cloth and just lay-on the gravel. Any weeds—they surely will appear—can simply be disturbed and uprooted by moving the gravel with a simple hoe or rake. The depth of the gravel will ensure that even the most pernicious weeds will never get a good toe-hold into viable soil.

What about all that extra soil generated by digging so deeply in the path, and terrace areas? Use it to create a vertical folly; or, after sifting, add the soil to your raised vegetable beds.

Back to the folly for a minute. In small, flat gardens, trellises with vines are a way to gain more space for plants. In addition, I have added more ground room in gardens by building up terraces with rough stones or other urban rubble. Into these constructs I have planted scree-loving alpines, drought-tolerant herbs, and perennials.

Every type of plant that relishes a good drainage location thrives in these follies. And the added height, even if it is only three stones high, or maybe grander in scale, adds a new, specialized habitat for experimentation.

Isn't that what we are all looking for?

June 1999

Through a Child's Eyes

IN THESE LAST FEW WEEKS, caps and gowns of all sizes have been donned and celebrations staged to mark one of life's passages. Perhaps now is the time to let youth step into the garden.

It's important for all of us to have our special place in a garden where no one else dares tread. We need to be able to pile stones and make flags, or let it all grow, including the weeds, if we want, with wild abandon.

The additional elements needed for a child's garden are to ensure the plants and soil are non-toxic, and that the new plantings will grow well. Shasta daisies, cosmos, and zinnias can provide a profusion of flowers. Zucchini and sunflowers are sure bets. Herbs provide scents that linger.

In the best of all possible worlds, the child's garden teaches about tools, sunlight, growth, water and how it moves, and the wonderful practice of keeping a journal with measurements and drawings. It can also teach the rest of us to see through their eyes.

A child's way of seeing has always brought me some very rich surprises and new insights. I also look back with great fondness to the memories of gardens I made as a child. In many ways, they still remain the best gardens I have ever made.

June 1995

Summer

There is a certain unexpected sweetness to the first light of day. Usually the air is perfectly still as the light strengthens; the sweet scent of the night's dampness is in the air; the birds start their carols, and the garden seems fresh with possibilities.

School's Out

AND THE CHILDREN ARE home all day.

One way to gain more time for yourself in the garden is to set aside a garden area for your children that is theirs, and theirs alone, to design, plant, weed, water, and harvest.

A sunny location away from shrub and tree roots will assure the best success—and a sure success is achievable.

Radishes, carrots, and sunflowers from seed make good choices. Potato and onion plants offer harvesting surprises later in the season. Herbs, such as chives, parsley, and oregano offer continual harvesting possibilities, and will be there for them next year. Flowers could include cosmos, nasturtiums, and zinnias. Bush beans offer the challenge of finding the beans.

Of course, zucchini is the all-time ideal plant for the novice. It is a successful plant under the most trying conditions. It covers a lot of ground quickly, and who can resist keeping one of its fruits on the vine until it reaches mammoth proportions?

If you shudder when contemplating the zucchini plant, then the pumpkin plant is a good fallback.

All of the plants mentioned above are known for being slug-resistant and generally bug-free—no scary, ugly green hornworms to pick off. And harvesting times can slide without loss of product.

Additionally, the harvest of flowers and herbs, along with the vegetables, can turn into a moment of pride for your child at those special summer dinners with friends and family.

June 1993

A Rose is Always a Rose

DESPITE OCCASIONAL RAIN and wind and persistent cloud cover, the first roses of June slowly close the door on spring's tentative and delicate raptures.

Sumer is icumen in, as the medieval English lyric has it. Summer has arrived.

Roses conjure myths and mysteries, serve as symbols of passion and evocative motifs within religious traditions, and festoon arbors and barns. There seems to be no other flower that has given us such a wealth of folklore, history, naming conventions, paintings, etchings, literature, and poetry.

In recent times, the plant has been forced into rigid symmetry within city rose gardens, while its wilder cousins have taken over abandoned cemetery plots. The rose has been known to grow so vigorously that arbors and barns have been overcome by its rampancy. We all have our vivid memories of roses gone wild.

There are gardeners who will not allow the rose into their garden, fearing its reputation as a high-maintenance plant, prone to preposterous diseases. A number of modern roses, accompanied by popular horticultural advice, do fulfill these prophecies.

However, the tide is turning: our local, general-interest nurseries are beginning to offer a much wider rose selection. The "old garden roses" and many species of roses have become popular and available, though in limited quantities. The English rose and its cultivars, often called David Austin roses, have become prevalent because they have been bred to look like the older roses to yield a pleasurable scent, to be repeat bloomers, and to offer greater disease resistance.

So, today I feel at ease suggesting that no garden should be without the pleasure of a rose.

Reading about the history of the rose becomes a study of the world—six of our seven continents have their own species of rose. It is from these wild roses that plant explorers and breeders, both amateurs and professionals, have made or contributed to the vast array of rose types known to us through paintings, history, and literature.

This history includes the rise and fall of kingdoms, war and peace, tales of mighty heroism, lifetimes of quiet determination, and the story continues today with the same vigor.

The classification and naming of roses continues to be in a state of flux, and the publication of books on roses continues unabated. Graham Stuart Thomas's books are the ones I started with, and have kept returning to, over these past two decades. Books by Peter Beales are beautifully instructive; in his most recent book, *Visions of Roses*, he writes about the multiple uses for the rose plant by taking us on a tour of thirty-three gardens, each beautifully photographed by Vivian Russell.

The Quest for the Rose, by Roger Phillips and Martyn Rix, is both a good, historical overview and a practical reference guide to a vast selection of roses. *The Love of the Rose,* by Graham Rose and Peter King, is an easily accessible and interesting cultural history of the rose.

Today my rose bouquet on my writing table includes *Rosa* 'Stanwell Perpetual', *Rosa moyesii, Rosa eglanteria, Rosa damascena,* and a rose I have dubbed Jerry's rose. Jerry's rose was given to me last year by an acquaintance; he no longer had room in his garden for this huge rose bush. Its sweetly scented, pink blooms have a faint white strip on each petal.

I look forward to the day when a rose expert tells me its true name; meanwhile, it continues to enchant me with its mystery and beauty.

Rosa 'Stanwell Perpetual' will continue to produce its exquisitely fragrant blooms all summer, and the *Rosa moyesii* will create spectacular rosehips this fall.

The *Rosa damascena* always comes perilously close to being removed from the garden, for it does get disfigured each year. However, as I look at the bloom's sensual blowsiness, think about its long, long history, and then breathe in its scent, I know that it will always have to be in my garden, along with its complement of chewing insects.

The *Rosa eglanteria* is a species rose from Europe that has naturalized throughout the world. The early American settlers used it extensively for protective hedges and screens. Aside from its practical uses, it has been grown for its dark-green, aromatic leaves which smell like apples, especially after rain.

Does this not tell us that this rose belongs in our Northwest garden?

June 1997

A Green Calm

A FRIEND WAS BEMOANING the lack of bloom continuity after the magnificent display had passed from his Shasta daisy and daffodil beds. It started me thinking about the current tyranny of the perennial border in our lives.

Do we need complex textures and colors always creating a riot of bloom? Could a leafy-green, calming pause bring pleasure to these warm days while we sit and enjoy the tranquility of the season?

Ferns can offer this leafy calm and are remarkably easy to grow. Underplant them with snowdrops; maybe then you will remember to clean up their old fronds, in order to see more clearly the emerging bulbs of January.

The daffodil blooms will be set off by the unfurling fronds; by planting the autumn-flowering cyclamen, wilting spring foliage can be hidden from view. The beds will have their four seasons of color, but most importantly, they will offer a summer-green calm. Surprisingly, the male fern (*Dryopteris filix-mas*) can thrive in a sunny bed if given deep waterings.

It's a magnificent fern which sends up a tall sheaf of fronds. It stands higher than our sword fern, which can also take the sun and has a more delicate, lighter green cast to its fronds.

Used in combination or alone, these ferns start to add an exotic quality to our garden spaces. Suddenly, you want to add a stone outcropping or perhaps a piece of sculpture, or a water jar. Best of all, they have taken your mind away from worrying about having color in the garden.

June 1995

Some Finer Touches

WHEN GRASS IS KEPT LONG, it grows faster. That makes sense when you think about those beautiful, long blades having so much surface to absorb the sunshine.

The point of all this is to keep the grass short if, in the final analysis, you want to slow its growth.

Also, if this year you want to stop irrigating and allow the grass to go dormant and golden in August, the grass will be in a healthier and sturdier condition. Additionally, it will withstand dormancy better if it hasn't expended a lot of energy growing vigorously, before being forced back into dormancy.

Other plants that could use some vigorous cutting back right now include tarragon, chives, and other herbs that may be getting leggy. Vigorous new growth will appear soon.

Your congested beds of bearded iris can be lifted and divided, now that the blooms are finished. The first great flush of blooms, whether they be roses or poppies or geraniums, need to be regularly deadheaded in order to encourage more blooms.

This is also true of any annuals.

And now is a good time to take softwood cuttings of camellias, daphne, mock orange, roses, or any of your favorite flowering shrubs and perennials. Try to take a wide variety of stem sizes, for there is no perfect diameter size that guarantees success. Strip off the leaves from the bottom three inches, pinch off the growing tip, and put the cuttings into a vegetable bed or at the back of a perennial bed.

This approach for making more plants is so much easier than trying to grow them in containers. The important consideration is to put them where they will get regular watering as they form new roots.

June 1996

The Garden Gives Back

THE STATISTICS THAT CONTINUE to be published show, with fancy charts, how gardening has become a multi-billion-dollar, American pastime.

I have yet to see any ruminations on why, beyond some words about the economic need to stay closer to home.

Could it possibly be a way to react to our culture, where the term "whatever" and a shrug often shape the conversational tone? Have we turned to the act of gardening as a refuge from the horrible realities in the news?

Growing up, I remember hearing the stories about Victory Gardens. Everyone, it seemed, felt compelled to make one. Besides growing food, did those gardens help their makers deal with World War II?

I know from my own experience that an evening spent tending my garden, after another incomprehensible day, brings a strength and calmness that no other activity can match. Are the qualities associated with gardening, such as nurturing, and the hard work of hands and heart, deficient in our culture? Much good writing has been done about the garden as a special place.

Forgive these musings. It just seemed time to reflect on why we, as a culture, are turning to gardening with such passion.

June 1995

Fourth of July is Behind Us

IT IS A BONUS TO HAVE the Fourth of July behind us, for now we can be confident that good weather and quieter days and nights await.

We may, fingers crossed, get red tomatoes this year. These recent warm days, however, wreak havoc with our container gardens. To maintain their lush growth, it is necessary to water in the morning, and again in the evening.

I have had great results with the smaller pots when I give them an overnight soaking: I put them into a tub of water up to their elbows. They have then absorbed enough water to expand the soil in that dry area between the soil and the pot. Containers can become a great joy for arranging the different forms, textures, and colors of a wide range of different plant types.

Pots with small shrubs, mixed with diverse pots of perennials, surrounded by profuse pots of annuals, can make an ever-changing tapestry in various garden locations. By having the different plants in their own pots, the problem of failure is avoided completely.

When I used to combine different plants into one pot, invariably it seemed that the key structural plant for each pot combination would decide to fail. Also, if the different height combinations need adjusting, adding a few more bricks to build up the pots' platform seems ever so much easier.

July 1994

A Starter Kit for the Little Ones

THE RASPBERRIES NEED CROPPING, the salad greens are prolific, and the garden's abundance declares it is high summer.

We are once again eating from our gardens, and nothing ever tastes better than food produced by our vigilance and care. So quickly we forget those low-lit, winter days, when we are immersed in summer's light and fertility.

For those of us who planned great garden projects this year, we have also reached a peak: we can no longer procrastinate, nor can we abandon all hope. The rest of summer beckons with long days. These days, the garden draws us away from other projects and schedules. And so, we must celebrate and revel in the fecundity.

It's still not too late to broadcast the seeds lying in their packets on the kitchen table—if we remember to keep them moist until germination. If the children or grandchildren seem interested in growing their own, give them the sure-fire seeds to start with: nasturtiums, arugula, sunflowers, and of course beans, which can be started with a damp paper towel in a glass on the windowsill.

Five days later, they are ready to be planted. Despite any daytime showers, the evenings are inevitably pleasant and dry. Sit for a while, listen to the birds chatter, and visit with neighbors or friends. Then take all those cookbooks outside and make notes, and mark the recipes we'll all need in just a few short weeks, when the rest of the garden is ready for its full-summer harvest.

July 1997

A Garden Walkabout

BEFORE THESE LIGHT-FILLED, early mornings turn dark again, make sure you take the time to indulge yourself in the experience of spending the day's waking hours in the garden.

There is a certain unexpected sweetness to the first light of day. Usually the air is perfectly still as the light strengthens; the sweet scent of the night's dampness is in the air; the birds start their carols and the garden seems fresh with possibilities.

It is a quiet time to move slowly, and to look closely. Soon, the first barking of a dog will be heard, and then somewhere a car door slams, and the semi-distant urban hum picks up. Somehow, though, that sweet time in the garden stays with you as the day progresses.

This is a good time to check the edges of your garden—what I call my walkabout. I walk around my garden in a pattern different from my daily comings and goings, in order to discover new areas of un-checked growth.

I invariably find that a shrub has overgrown the electric meter; a tree branch is in the way of sidewalk pedestrians; a hazelnut shrub has discovered the plea-sures of my roof gutters.

It also becomes apparent that some areas of the garden can grow quite vigorously on their own—even in charming ways.

July 1994

Hail the Wild Strawberry

IT SEEMS HARD TO BELIEVE that some of our garden crops have already finished.

Strawberries are done, unless you have planted a variety that promises to fruit past June. Perhaps you have found the wonders of the alpine strawberry, variously called *fraises des bois*, wild strawberry or woodland strawberry.

These plants fruit prodigiously from spring to fall. I have seen them referred to as a "novelty" plant and passed off as incapable of providing a meal-size serving. Obviously, the author of that point of view never tasted the pure essence of their berries at the end of a long day.

I plant mine right by the front door, and enjoy a handful of berries on the way to work and at the end of the day. I was out of town last week, and came home to find the plants laden with fruit; in fact, more than a meal-size serving.

The variety called 'Baron Solemacher' turns into a very handsome cluster of dark- green leaves with simple white flowers and berries borne above the leaves.

It does not produce runners, but it can be divided easily from the center, and it makes a fine edging plant.

They need to be planted about eighteen inches apart in the spring. Give your favorite nursery a call. They may still have some plants available for this year. Cut the leaves back hard to force the new growth from the center. They do well with an eastern exposure; they will fail if planted in the full, afternoon sun.

It's such a wonderful plant. The more you eat, the more it produces.

July 1993

Winter Vegetables Now?

AS WE SAVOR OUR JUICY, sweet, succulent strawberries, revel in the fresh arugula, push the basil along and dream about a ripe tomato, it just seems incongruous that we should be planning and planting our winter garden vegetables now. And by the way, just where in the lush, full overgrowth of the summer vegetable garden do we install the seeds and starts?

Winter vegetables include mixed winter greens (kales, Asian greens, mustards), potatoes, winter leeks, and fava beans. By combining these with the prolific summer squash (pureed and frozen), your winter soups will have pride of place at the table, and your household food budget will show some significant savings. A friend has kept meticulous production records. She calculates a savings rate of between $300 and $400 for a two-person household. This is just from the winter vegetables.

Additionally, there is the pride in knowing that you have reduced transportation costs and fuel.

So, where to plant becomes the consuming question. With the summer heat settling in, your springtime, leafy vegetables are goners. Out they go. There, that makes a nice big space, even though the neat and colorful lettuce rows added a nice design element.

Some of the lengthy trailers on the squash plants can be removed, or artfully corralled into smaller spaces. A bit later this month, the tomato plants should be heavily pruned. All new, flowering branches should be removed, and much of the leafy growth reduced in volume. This opens the plants to the sunshine. It also focuses the plants' energy on the fruit that has set.

Find out about the volunteer activities at your local P-Patch. Knowledgeable vegetable gardeners, who are often noted for being always ready to dispense advice, will surround you.

All of this planning and planting may feel overwhelming and not worth the trouble. But the big payoff comes in the winter. Winter vegetables only need to be cropped. There is no need to water. Weeds are non-existent, and slugs are not a problem.

July 2006

After the Rains, Things to Do

FINALLY, THE SUN IS SHINING on our gardens.

Those annual plants that have suffered from our wet July should probably be removed, and the bare spots replanted with a fast-growing seed, like arugula or some bedding-out plants from your favorite nursery.

The aphid-infested shrubs and flowers can be cleaned up with a strong blast from the garden hose. For individual blooms, hold your hand behind the flower stalk while you blast it with water. Most of the aphids will be blown off and you can repeat the process next week for the final removal of these critters.

Cut back the tired blossoms of your annuals and perennials. They will respond with better growth. Begin to cut your herbs and flowers for drying, and make sure your drying areas are well ventilated this year. When the days have been warm and dry, set the height on your mower to three inches in order to prevent scorching. And then water deeply.

In spite of the recent rains, the soil may be bone dry beneath your deciduous and evergreen trees and shrubs. Set the sprinklers in the morning hours, and let them soak the earth for at least an hour. Watch for any undue runoff, for that means the soaking is not taking place.

You may have to take a measured approach and water for ten minutes the first day, and then twenty minutes the next day, until the soil has opened up again to accept a deep watering.

Doing so will prepare your plants nicely for the afternoon heat.

July 1993

A Time to Pause

THE RUSH OF ATTENDING this year's garden has started to slow, accompanied, perhaps, by a sense of some success, and also the more familiar sense of frustration.

The bare spots still protrude, and the integrated, pest-management system seems to have provided a luxurious breeding ground for new, unique, actively chewing and spotting organisms.

The beauty of the rose is fading, and the vegetables seem to have stopped growing. It is indeed a time to pause and rethink the garden.

This should be a time and place for discovery and pleasure, not the occasion to worry over, or compete with the latest expert advice. More than a lifetime of learning is involved with the making and tending of a garden.

The leaf drop now cluttering our paths and beds comes from two sources this year. It is in July that the broadleaf evergreens, such as the madrona and strawberry tree, naturally drop last year's leaves. The first time one becomes aware of this mid-summer leaf clutter, it brings the dread of having done something wrong—especially in the too-much or too-little watering category. What a wonderful sense of relief comes with the knowledge that this is supposed to happen in July every year.

July 1995

Plant Now for the Fall-Winter Kitchen Garden

WITH THE FULLNESS AND HEAT of summer upon us, it's almost impossible to think about starting our cool season crops now. Of course, the first question that leaps to the fore is: Where do we find room to start more plants?

It is the wise gardener who knows to leave a bare area that gets only the morning sun; this is the seedbed for cool-season vegetables.

Here's a short list for fall and winter crops or crops started now for over-wintering:

> *Lettuce*: sow in early August; transplant in October
>
> *Onions*: sow in early August; transplant in December/January
>
> *Spring cabbage*: sow in late August; transplant in November/January
>
> *Spring cauliflower*: sow in mid-July; transplant in October/November
>
> *Winter scallions*: sow in mid-July; transplant in mid-October

So much of the available literature emphasizes the garden harvest of summer and early fall. However, we're fortunate to live in a climate mild enough to allow us to continue to harvest from our gardens year-round.

I have been slow to learn about cool-season crops, due to my utter failure to understand that I could make room in my garden for a series of nursery beds facing east, where I could grow these crops. A wonderful sense of continuity comes in, filling up the cleared summer-vegetable beds with these seedlings. It gives a reassurance that the garden will still produce, once we begin our migration from the garden toward the hearth.

Planning and preparation for the cool, short days of autumn and winter take considerable discipline during the heat of summer.

July 1995

Time for Autumn Bulbs

MY HEART WENT OUT to the bikers and campers when the rains came early on Sunday morning, but what a blessed, wet sound. The garden, having been beaten down by the recent heat wave, could once again breathe freely and be a place of beauty and optimism.

Now that we have been given a moment to pause and reflect in the great, gray coolness of a Northwest summer day, the lists of things to be done in the garden can be looked at again.

It's time to find room to plant the autumn bulbs. The autumn crocus (*Colchicum autumnale*) is often recommended, but I find its foliage, which comes after the flower, to be a coarse and troublesome presence. A true crocus of autumn—and it is hard to differentiate except by counting the stamens—is *Crocus speciosus*. It's easy to grow, and has a light foliage that offers no hint of vulgarity. Several charming varieties have been developed, which give pure colors, such as 'Alba' (white) and 'Conqueror', a deep, sky-blue variety.

Nerine bowdenii is a South African bulb which offers its pink, lacy, trumpet-shaped flowers for a long bloom period in September and October. It needs well-drained, relatively dry soil to thrive.

By far my favorite is *Sternbergia* for its vibrant, intense yellow, crocus-like flowers. The color seems so appropriate to the season. *Sternbergia lutea* is the most common form, and once it is established in a sunny location it will flower for years.

July 1995

To Watch the Wind

IT'S TOO HOT TO DIG, but the early morning hours have become a fine time to be in the garden.

It feels like the world is yours and yours alone, except for the early morning neighborhood cat patrols, and the wonderful chatter of the birds safely in the trees. Some extraordinary growth has been going on in the least-visited areas of the garden. This is a good time to "walk the edges" of the garden with a small saw, sharp loppers, and trusty pruners.

It's important to remember that other people, such as the gas and water meter readers and your neighbors, have a different relationship to your garden.

Aside from tending the vegetable garden, the early summer perennials need their faded blooms removed, and the late-summer annuals and perennials may need staking and tidying.

Seizing the early or late hours of the day makes the time spent in the garden less hurried and stressful. It's the perfect time for watering, and the work seems to be more productive than starting in the heat of the day.

When the early morning hours are cut short by other activities, your mind is filled with thoughts about what still needs to be done, so that going back out to the garden in the evening you know exactly where to start once the sprinklers have finished.

And then there is that quiet time to just enjoy the garden. It's not a time to think about perfection, or have idle dreams of grandeur. It is a time to sit quietly and watch the wind move in the leaves. And remember the delight you had as a child when you picked a flower.

July 1996

A Glass of Wine

IT FELT LIKE THE GARDEN was Northwest-damp again, after last week's unseasonably cold and rainy weather.

However, the soil is very dry under hedges and trees, for the rain was neither strong, nor voluminous enough, to penetrate any covering on the soil. This includes areas that have a good summer mulch cover. With the return of the warm, summer weather, be sure to thoroughly irrigate the entire garden except, perhaps, the golden-colored lawn.

If you have soaker hoses, check their functional cover. Often, earwigs and other critters take up residence in the coolth of the irrigation system and block the water outflow. You may think that water is getting to all the areas, but a systematic reality check may prove otherwise.

Currently, the broadleaf evergreens are shedding last year's leaves; this is not a sign of drought or disease, but rather the normal functioning of these plants.

Azaleas, rhododendrons, and other non-needle type evergreen will drop last year's leaves in July. When I first saw this trait my heart stopped, for I thought it was an abnormal, early-fall leaf drop. Now I look at this July leaf cleanup as early job training for the fall leaf drop from the deciduous trees and shrubs.

These July days bring a fullness of flowers, the dappled light of shade, and the promise of an abundant harvest. As for that bare spot where nothing got planted or survived, try planting radish and arugula seeds. They both germinate in ten days.

The arugula flowers are pungently perfect for late summer salads. Radish slices with cold butter on them, together with French bread and a glass of wine, allow one to sit down and enjoy the soft, warm summer air and the fruits of our garden work.

July 1996

Three Shade Trees

EVERYONE SHOULD HAVE a shade tree to gaze up into on these hot summer days.

Looking through the branches at the filtered light brings a calm and mesmerizing feeling that makes the discomfort of the heat evaporate into the surrounding haze.

Acer palmatum, the Japanese maple, can become a perfect shade tree for sitting under, if a cultivar is chosen that promises to become a thirty to fifty-foot specimen. While that may sound too over-scaled for our small city lots, do remember that the chances of it ever becoming fifty feet in your lifetime remain slim to none.

Many Japanese maple cultivars can be shrubby and low in habit, but by judicious pruning to just three main branches above the trunk, and pruning the center to be open, the desired effect can be achieved in your lifetime.

Another beautiful and rugged tree that is often overlooked is the snowbell tree, *Styrax japonicus*. Again, it is necessary to prune the young tree to grow into a prized and perfectly shaped shade tree. The *Styrax* has an early proclivity towards shrubbiness, but by guiding the trunk and three main branches, it grows on with little or no care.

Finally, the Chinese scholar tree, *Sophora japonica*, should be considered. Again, here is a trouble-free tree, for it is capable of fixing nitrogen in the ground. Therefore, it can thrive in very poor conditions.

The *Sophora* and the *Styrax* both have white flowers in May, and all three trees display beautiful fall colors.

Other important considerations for choosing these trees include their lack of attraction for sucking insects and caterpillars, in addition to their robust and easy cultivation. Nor do they carry fruits or heavy seed pods that might drop on your head during your warm, summer reveries.

July 1996

Books in the Garden

RATHER THAN SEEKING ANSWERS or advice on "issues" in the garden, I turn to books this time of year with the hope of unknown discovery. This is the time to seize these days of languor, and drift into uncharted territories.

Here are some suggestions for the perfect, garden -related book of August.

Cascadia Wild, edited by M. Friedman and P. Lind-holdt, speaks of ecosystems and politics, while *Talking on the Water* by Jonathan White is about conversations that ultimately link together the sense of community and nature.

The poetic beauty of Maxine Kumin's essays and stories in *Women, Animals and Vegetables* might very well send you searching for her poetry. Odds are George Schenk's *Gardening with Friends* will produce audible laughter among those who normally don't laugh—maybe only smile—while reading.

A must-read is Sara Stein's bestseller *Noah's Garden.* Stein casts an appraising eye on the ecology of our own back yards while advocating for the use of native plants. Any of Allen Lacy's collections of essays will bring you back to thinking about the wide, wonderful world of plants that might, and perhaps should, find their way into your plans for next year's garden.

One of my favorite books is by Anne Raver, *Deep in the Green, An Exploration of Country Pleasures,* a collection of essays previously published in *Newsday* and *The New York Times.* It is a wonderful trove. As she explains in her introduction, these essays aren't about the specifics of making a garden, but "making connections." And, "It's about the joy of obsession. It's about friends...It tells the story of the earthworm...It's about growing old." And, most pointedly, Raver tells us, "It's about losing things you love...it is about going on." Raver's essays have given me great insights into new thoughts and new ways of looking at the efforts I put forth in my garden.

Meanwhile, I am working through Vita Sackville West's garden books with the greatest of pleasure.

August 1995

At the Helm of a Beautiful Yacht

THESE ARE THE DOG DAYS of summer, a time to make pleasant listlessness a habit.

It's too early for serious pruning or transplanting, and we have probably already picked our ripe vegetables.

However, this is a good time to turn to our camellia bushes. The bushes have set their buds for next spring and, if you look closely, you will see from two to five buds bunched together. Carefully snap off all but one bud at the end of these clusters and your plant will thrive and look better next spring.

While this is a tedious job, it can be made much more pleasant by doing a little of the cropping of the buds each day for ten minutes. Additionally, the warmth of the days lends themselves to standing still in the garden, whereas doing a job like this in the chill of the next season only leads to cold fingers and backsides.

Stroll around your garden with a notepad and tape measure. Is this the year to replace that narrow, broken walkway you use every week to roll out the garbage can? It's hard to describe the sheer pleasure I experience each week as I use my new walkway.

Originally, it was twenty-four inches wide—just as wide as the wheelbase of the heavy monthly recycling bin. The path was cracked, and had been lifted by tree roots, making for little bumps that threw the big bin off into the garden beds. My new walkway is thirty inches wide and smooth as silk.

As I roll my cans to the curb each week, I feel as though I were at the helm of the world's most beautiful yacht.

August 1993

Beyond the Flowers: the "Bones" of Your Garden

BRAVO, AND MY HIGHEST and best salutes to all those garden constructionists out there.

I am talking about those gardeners who lay the paths, construct the terraces, build the arbors, and design and install the irrigation and lighting systems.

Without some or all of these elements, all the flowers in the world won't add up to a garden. These are the "bones" of a good garden, as shown so clearly by the famous garden in Japan, *Ryoan-ji*, with its walls that enclose and rocks placed carefully on sand.

The early gardens of Islam were enclosed by walls and contained a cross-pattern of water channels. Of course, they grew fruit trees and flowers, but the lasting image of these gardens are the walls and water channels.

As guests are invited into the garden to be shown special plants, how would they be able to see them up close without the system of paths that have been developed? And how does one keep the garden itself from spilling onto the neighbors below without having walls?

Unless these elements are made from expensive materials, visitors so often overlook them. Always, it seems, the focus is on the flowers, when in fact the sense of being in a great garden really has to do with the sense of the garden having been made.

As the vegetables try to ripen during these cool days, look again at how your garden is constructed. Think about the "bones" of your garden.

August 1996

Mid-August...Relax

MID-AUGUST CAN BE a pleasantly quiet time in the garden. It is just a bit too early to renovate the lawn, or to dig and divide the perennials, and the weeds have lost their vigor to turn up in hordes overnight.

Yet there are still plenty of tasks to keep the gardener feeling like a useful citizen; it is just that the work can be kept to a slow, summertime pace.

On warm summer evenings, it is a pleasure to weed a garden bed right after it has been watered. It becomes a good way to check on how thorough or accurate the irrigation has been, and also a time when the weeds come out of the refreshingly cool, damp earth with ease.

By removing the spent flowers on your perennials at this time, there may be a chance for more blooms this year in the vegetable and herb beds. The apples, pears, and peaches have started to ripen, but not yet in such vast quantities that we have to think about canning jars. The houseguests haven't stayed too long, yet, and maybe they even want to help in the garden. The current tasks of watering, weeding, and harvesting can safely be given over to their care, whatever their level of talent or age.

I hope you are enjoying the slower pace; it is a time to put aside the hopes for garden perfection, and revel in all that the garden does produce, whether that be shade trees, wonderful produce, or just a place to be.

August 1994

Could This Be...

SUMMERTIME?

As I write this column there is still a gray, foggy chill in the air. Yes, we have been allowed a few brief moments of sunshine later in the afternoon, but the chill returns at dusk. However, according to "them that know," in just a few days...when you read this... the afternoon temperature will be hovering in the mid-eighties.

How can a dedicated gardener cope with all of these crazy, summertime weather fluctuations? Patience helps, but a wicked sense of humor is also critically important.

These last few days of cool weather and fog have put a dent in the forward progression of our heat-loving crops, but the beans seem to be in overdrive, and of course the squash plants are producing jumbo-scaled veggies overnight. Beans are easy to blanch and freeze, but the squash plants always require further referencing for interesting recipes.

For the winter squash and the pumpkins, their newly emerged fruits should have a piece of wood placed under them, so that their skins will not be rotted by the damp soil. For those tomato plants with their exuberant growth bursting out of their cages, the lower shoots should be pruned off entirely in order to keep the soil-borne diseases at bay. Additionally, prune off all side-shoots so that the energy of the plant can be focused on both the main growth stem and those tiny, round, green nubbins that we all hope will be ripe tomatoes soon. Some knowledgeable urban farmers cut off the new blossoms about this time, so that again energy can be directed to the fruits that have already set.

Your open vegetable and fruit tree beds do get a thorough soaking from your irrigation systems. However, do check the soil under your deciduous trees and shrubs, and your evergreen shrubs. In spite of the cool, gray weather, the evaporation factor is still at its summertime rate.

I was stunned to find some rhododendrons seriously drooping with drama. I had given that corner of the garden a serious, long soak just five days before. Then I started to check other supposedly well-irrigated sites in the garden, and realized that the cool and damp days had lulled me into gravely miscalculating my watering schedules. Fortunately, the plants seem to be forgiving my trespasses, so far.

As a reminder, I use water pots throughout my garden. These elegant urns get topped-off every other day, so the mosquito larvae are always washed away. I continue to be amazed at how low their water levels become in such short periods of time.

I love to see the trees and sky reflected in their still waters, and the birds that sip at their edges. Additionally, there are neighborhood cats that straddle these pots and drink at length. These cats always appear to me as mighty lions coming to the watering hole during the heat of the day.

This evening, with a light sweater wrapped around my shoulders, I watch with joy the summer light lingering for deliciously long hours. I contemplate the "threat" of summer heat coming our way. I've decided that I can hardly wait for its arrival.

August 2010

Take Heart with Species Bulbs

AS THE SUMMER HARVESTING CONTINUES, thoughts of spring arise as the first bulb catalogues arrive in our mailboxes.

If you find yourself looking at brightly colored pictures of vast seas of big daffodils or tulips with dread, remembering all the money and effort spent for what turned out to be a miserable spring showing, take heart and search the catalogues for their offerings of species bulbs.

The species tulips, narcissi and crocus bulbs are almost always hardier than their hybrid cousins, and while they produce smaller flowers, the blooms tend to be in greater abundance, and they last longer.

The bulbs grow lower to the ground, which is a blessing here in the Northwest, due to the late winter and early spring squalls that come galloping through our gardens.

My early-flowering crocuses have emerged from a blanket of snow without a sign of storm damage. This hardiness truly amazes me, especially as I look at the hybrid crocus, which often turns to mush after a heavy rainfall.

Most bulb catalogues and local nurseries have started to supply the species bulbs along with the standard, large-flowering hybrids. I encourage you to try the species bulbs this year. Remember, when you are arranging them in your garden, the scale is much smaller than the hybrids. Try, for example, to inter-plant the common, small grape hyacinth, *Muscari arme-niacum,* to achieve a greater massing for the first year.

August 1994

Trees Can Also Bring Neighbors Together

A PAUSE BEFORE THE BUSY WORK that needs to be done in the garden during the autumn season.

When I took a walk in the neighborhood today with some students of mine, I threw out the red-herring statement that the landscapes in the "better" parts of our community felt better because the homeowners planted trees.

I was accosted—that's the proper word—with statements maintaining that there were only three households per block, instead of eighteen. Upon reflection, I am going to stay with that premise, with a few caveats tossed in.

Yes, there is more space between the homes in my part of the world, and the lot sizes are large enough to accept major tree plantings. However, we can all work with our neighbors on smaller and denser lot sizes, and achieve a greater green scale for our surrounding landscape.

I have been working with the neighbors across the street, and with their permission have planted five new street trees, in addition to the eight street trees planted last year.

The streetscape is starting to become unified, and speaks to the concept of developing a sense of place. In five years, or so, this block will be home to a sensibility that echoes the city's great boulevards, with their stately old trees.

In seems a small effort in the larger framework of the ongoing efforts to re-green our cities, but the experience of working with my neighbors, learning about their landscape ideas, and sharing some fine stories and bad jokes, has been every bit as valuable to me as the lovely, new plantings.

August 1994

Summer's Vantage Point

SO, MAYBE YOU DIDN'T PLANT tropicals this year, and therefore you're feeling your garden has no charm.

Or, you went on a number of garden tours and shopping expeditions, and now the collection of plants that you tucked in has created a potpourri of confusion that falls short of your garden vision.

Or, we are pulled into our gardens to stake the toppling lilies, or to prune the tangling vines out of the shrubbery. Suddenly we spot areas of extreme dryness. While setting the sprinkler, we try to remember where we put the folder with all the information about pruning and insect control.

The tender expectancy of spring is but a distant memory. Question: should our gardens really become such all-consuming worries and checklists of tasks? In our current, over-hyped, and frenetic culture, too much information bombards us; it is easy to be swept away into believing we can take it all in and act upon it.

Maybe you even want to stop reading right here, for that matter. Or, you could make a fresh batch of lemonade. Or, better, let summer seep into your bones.

Trees have always played a key role in summer, not only for shade, but also as places in our youth where we climbed and hid out in, or looked up through the leaves to the blue sky in wonder.

So often in urban settings, we plant only small trees. Yet, maybe we miss our larger trees, and wonder how we can fit them in again. Sharing a tree on the property line certainly allows for greater scale. It also requires a neighborly dialogue, which in many ways has become as much a memory as our grand trees.

As adults, we also need to let the long, summer days quiet us within. Reading a book, rather than trying to plow through that huge stack of unread magazines, can bring a calming, yet exhilarating sense of letting time pass through us, rather than controlling us.

Barry Lopez's writing has always put me into a dreamlike state, and his collection of essays, *About This*

Life, has been issued in paperback. These essays take us around the world and into worlds; here is a naturalist asking some of the big questions of our age, and for the first time letting us into his life and personal thoughts.

His essays are the perfect summer reading—they take us on journeys. Remember those summers when you read outside until it got too dark? Lopez has written: "No one can fathom what happens between a human being and written language."

That mysteriously personal relationship is the perfect metaphor for our relationship with our gardens. Or with our summer memories.

If we can pause long enough for those memories to return, then the richness of the smell of lavender being picked, or the tangy, piney scent of tomato leaves under our touch, will overcome our worries about our non-tropical looking garden.

The tropicals can wait until next year. Or a lifetime.

August 1999

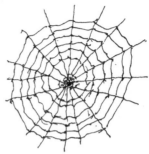

Dusty, Webby August

THE SOFT AND WARM, early morning air draws one out to the garden while your sleepy-winkers are still in place. Suddenly... a spider web grabs your face. Arms flail, hands smack your face and hair—and the charm of these fleeting summer days goes down a major notch. Later in the day, when the sun slants at a late summer angle, one can appreciate the extraordinary web constructs, but only the ones that are off your garden paths.

The garden is dusty, even in the shade. Spring's verdant newness has grown tired through these past months. The rains in July hid this passage, but now the leaves look wrinkled, their colors look less strong, and a few leaves have dared to show their autumn color.

However, smack dab in the midst of this dusty-webby scene is the vibrancy of the harvest. The sunflowers are standing tall, the tomatoes are showing great promise, the squash vines are cascading, or rampaging through, and bursting out from their formerly tidy spaces. The beans need to be picked every day, morning and night. And somewhat ironically, your perennials need to be propagated.

Yes, this is the time to take cuttings of your favorite woody plants, and make little sticks that will later in the year become plants in their own right. Your favorite lavender or viburnum, French tarragon, rose or rosemary? The list is probably bigger than your garden.

There are many theories and rules about propagating woody plants, that I was fortunate to learn from a wise Irishman. He had three rules: 1) Do not use tough woody parts; 2) Do not use tender, new growth; 3) Make many, many cuttings, and at this time of the year put them straight into the ground, where you will be watering your late-summer plants. In addition, cut back the growing tip, strip the bottom third of its leaves, and plunge the seven-inch cutting straight into the ground. He was a betting man, and he figured that if he took ten cuttings, he would harvest between five or seven viable plants in the late fall or early winter.

Years ago, for a wonderful client, I made what came to be called my stick garden. I had made all the paths, and defined the planting beds, and then did the planting. It was all cuttings! Yes, little sticks. Three months later people were asking about the names for the different plants and where I had sourced them. They wondered about the size of the budget that could support such a lush and intricate planting scheme.

My father taught me that you can, in fact, propagate roses from cuttings. I was dubious, but over the years I have succeeded, in spite of my misgivings. Of course, now the problem is where to plant my successes. There is one particular hardy rose I had seen in an alley. Each year it courageously scrambled higher into a laurel hedge, always throwing its sweet and tender pink blooms out into the blazing western exposure. Wow! I am still trying to find a place for my successful cutting in my garden. I am not on an alley, and I do not have a laurel hedge, nor do I have an equivalent, sturdy structure for all of its amazing vigor. Yet I do know that there will be a fine home for it, somewhere.

The garden pulls us around many bends, never behaving perfectly, always bringing surprises, and oftentimes sheer delight, especially when we stay quiet and let it inform us. During these last, few days of summer, all the garden really asks us to do is to crop and irrigate. The propagation stuff can happen next month, along with the bulb orders.

August 2012

Fully Loaded August Gardens

YES, THESE LAST FEW WEEKS we have been inundated with early offers from our favorite bulb catalogues and websites. The heart swoons as we think about the spring treasures to come next year.

Then one steps back, but of course only after submitting our dream orders, realizing the craziness of it all. Here in the heat and fullness of August we are planning for next spring's flowers? Once again, we can acknowledge that gardeners know no shame.

The people who work as addiction specialists haven't found us yet in their research, but we certainly might fall within their criteria. This year I am after allium bulbs, after seeing a heart-stopping display this year in England. Their bright globes bring such a wonderful vertical element.

The bulb purveyors want an amazing fortune for each *Allium* 'Globemaster' bulb. I think three will be quite enough. However, there is a remarkable range of other allium bulbs—and I want to try some of the more demure ones, especially for their contrast to the other big and colorful attention-getters.

Do read the fine print however, for several of the allium bulb descriptions state that the bulbs naturalize very rapidly. Another way to read this is to say they spread like a wildfire. That can be good news or bad news, depending upon your garden space. I wish my snowdrops, said to naturalize well, would spread like a wildfire.

I have dealt with plant invaders over the years in my garden. Some will never be eradicated (*Acanthus*) while others, with due diligence, will become lost to history. If your garden is a place for you to become lost to all cares, then an invasive plant can become an old friend, and your dueling natures will bring quiet amusement.

Now, back to the present. We all know that our productive gardens need to be cropped every day. Should a day pass without cropping, the sweet, small zucchinis will have taken on gigantic proportions, the tomatoes will have over-ripened, while the bush beans will be dragging their tails in the soil.

Aside from batches of zucchini bread for the freezer, there are many recipes for *Ratatouille Provençale*, which is a wonderful mixture of eggplant, zucchini, tomatoes, onion, garlic (lots of garlic for me), and in some recipes—peppers. This is all stewed together with good olive oil. Some say, in the end, it looks like a Braque still life.

There is nothing better during the deepest, darkest, coldest months of winter, when you can bring this out, re-heat, place a fresh poached egg on top, and smother it with grated parmesan cheese and freshly ground pepper. The warm, summer memories come flooding back. Adapt a recipe to make your own version, and eventually you can make a pot of *ratatouille* with totally different balances of ingredients, based upon your harvesting.

In the meantime, we have only a few more weeks of mild and benign weather. Let's look at the light, feel the warmth on our shoulders, and delight in the bounty that comes from the healthy earth.

August 2013

Summer Dwindles: Not Quite Yet, Please

I BLANDLY OPENED the front door to go out the other day, and lying right in front of me was a single, perfectly formed maple leaf announcing the fall season.

Its center was canary-yellow, while its outer edges were still a pure green. There was no browning on its edges, and there was no curl in its contours. It just laid there, in all its sturdiness, an item with heavy, provocative symbolism. Yes, it jarred me out of my blandness. Our warm, summer idyll would soon be over.

I pondered and looked around for other signs, but could find nothing as powerful as this single leaf. I brought it inside and thought to press it into a book, in order to remember how it had so startled me. And then the next few days were spent, in idle moments, pondering how we go along, expecting that nothing will change, and then either world events, family news, or a fall into a pothole can change what we so blithely take for granted, as we charge full steam ahead through our daily lives.

Soon there will be the chill in the air, and the trees will festoon themselves in brilliant colors; there will be that moment when the amount of leaves on the ground appears to be the same as on the trees, and the horizon line will briefly disappear in this riot of color. But right now, I want to stop time. I want the summer warmth. I want to cling to the summer memories—the old ones, and the new ones being made. I plan to blithely ignore the next leaf that has the cheekiness to place itself directly in my pathway.

August 2006

An Indelible Image

AH, WHAT LATE SUMMER IMAGES from a neighborhood sidewalk the other day: a woman wearing a new, fall suit beneath an open umbrella, followed by a woman in summer clothes enjoying an ice cream cone in the soft rain.

The first fall colors are showing, while we continue to hope for the red to arrive in our tomatoes. The garden is full of mature foliage and flowers, with a few tenacious weeds hiding in the fullness.

This is a good time to sweep through our gardens with pruners and trowel, digging out the weeds while cutting back the spent foliage and flowers. Do this cleanup work before the fall leaf-drop, and it becomes much easier to just rake and collect the fall leaves for a compost pile. By separating the leaves from the other garden materials, you can make a rich and loamy leaf mold compost.

This, too, is a transition time to celebrate. And the nurseries always have spectacular sales.

September 1996

Of Tomatoes and Roses

WE PLANT OUR SMALL TOMATO seedlings when the roses start to bloom freely. And so, we can harvest our tomatoes, and pick roses again, if we have roses that continue to bloom through the harvest season.

Rosa chinensis mutabilis, known as the butterfly rose, is blooming profusely again, after quieting down during August. This China rose continuously produces single flowers, with pale, yellow buds opening to show pale, pink petals, which then mature to a rich magenta. A full bush in a breeze looks like a butterfly collection.

Rosa 'Stanwell Perpetual,' a long-ignored cross between *Rosa damascena bifera* and *Rosa pimpinellifolia,* has lost favor due to its shrubby, lanky growth. However, if properly placed in the garden, you will value it for its scent despite its prickly, and sometimes shabby, mottled leaves.

Rosa moschata nastarana, the Persian Musk rose, has small, white buds, flushed with pink, growing in a cluster. This is a vigorous and hardy rose, which brings an elusive scent that just doesn't seem to be exactly right there—but is.

Imagine a basket filled with vine-ripened tomatoes, a zucchini or two, and three special roses gracing the top. It seems almost too good to be true.

September 1996

Not Ready Yet

WE KNEW IT HAD TO HAPPEN.

Some of us even spoke openly about wanting it to happen. But now that the weather has changed—from warm, beautiful, and sunny to significantly gray and one dimensional, I feel a little shocked and disheartened! Summer is almost over. I thought I was ready, but obviously not.

But here we are today, with a sunny afternoon, azure skies and fresh snow on the Olympic Mountains.

Now I remember why I have always loved the autumn season. The brisk air, and the yellows and reds of our deciduous trees swirling throughout our damp landscapes make the shortening days lively and vigorous.

I find the timing of this weather shift to be remarkable. Even though the neighborhood children had to return to school last week, it still felt and acted like summer. There was still the summer's sultry warmth, and the week was a short one due to the long Labor Day (and sunny and warm) weekend. Some of the kids were allowed to wear special outfits for the first days of school, and the backpacks and papers and pens were sort of like old friends, even if they were in some cases new. It was a week of beginnings, and there was a soft, summer slowness to all the changes.

Now this week there starts to be a new urgency. The playtime is over. Assignments need to get done. The pace is quickening. The cool bite of the marine air does help to bring a sharper focus.

The transitions that occur in the early autumn season seem to push and pull us, at times back towards brief remembrances of summer's soft warmth but always indefatigably forward into the chills of winter. Today I am putting up a kicking and screaming resistance towards that forward motion! The memories of summer are still quite fresh.

September 2003

Shutting Down

WITH THE RECENT COOL and incessant rains, this
year's growing season has shut down. Not entirely, of
course, for that would be too simple. But the push
towards a late harvest has significantly slowed. While
the damp air and soil have been a boon for some of our
ornamental shrubs and perennials, I sense that our
trees, both native and otherwise, are confused.

Why are my *Sisyrinchium striatum* blooming again
along with a rhododendron? And though at first I
thought they must be plastic, no, there were actually
fresh wisteria blooms on a neighbor's vine. I watch my
maple trees, coloring up briefly, stopping their prog-
ress towards their fiery autumnal displays. Summer's
dry leaves litter the landscape, but there is no real autumnal display of color. Too early you say? Yes, but the
summer harvest has stopped.

All of this year has been curious, to say the least.
I see some spectacular gardens, filled with bountiful
fruit and vegetable crops, but I also hear about many
neighbors saddened and frustrated by their less-than-
fruitful gardens. Some weatherman will hopefully
explain all of these weather anomalies to us at some
point, but meanwhile we find our gardens in a state
mostly unknown to us.

Do we start clearing out the summer detritus,
even though there might be another crop of beans, or
a small, tasty cucumber or a wimpy, but still yellow,

sunflower? Will our winter squashes fulfill their promise, or turn to mush while we await their peak of perfection?

I bring up all these questions, not to frustrate or confuse the novice or accomplished gardener, but to support us all. I have never seen such a confusing season and year. Last year we were seared by unusual and intense heat after a prolonged and intense cold spell in December. I think many of our trees, shrubs, and perennials were readjusting this year to last year's extremes. And then this year, a cold, wet spring was followed by intense spikes in summer temperatures within a less-than-warm summertime. I am confused, along with my beloved plants.

I will cut back spent blooms of lavender and francoa. I will tidy up my ferns where the maple and stewartia leaves will fall. What I mean by tidying up is to cut the low-lying fronds, so that when I scoop up a handful of brilliantly colored fall leaves, there will not be trailing fern fronds in the way. I will cut back any overgrowth on my hardscape paths, so that when I rake or sweep the fall leaves the edges will be clear. But it is all so tentative.

In three or four weeks it will all be so obvious. I will be on a mission to clean up the slowly rotting exuberance of the summer harvest, mulch and prepare the vegetable beds for the winter crops, plant all the treasures bought at the fall plant sales, transplant the trees, shrubs, and perennials that earlier this year ended up in the wrong place, and order spring bulbs.

September 2010

Nearing the Equinox

OUR GARDENS ARE BONE DRY, dusty, thirsty, and pa-
tiently waiting for the refreshment of the autumnal
rains. Yes, we can water or irrigate them, but the
end-of-summer dryness maintains a chokehold. I am
always amazed by how well the garden continues to
withstand the heat this time of year.

Many dry leaves rustle in the trees and on the
ground, yet the brilliant fall colors have not appeared.
Our plants seemed revitalized a few weeks ago with the
first touch of cool air, but the overall sense of deep
dustiness has returned, along with the midday heat.

As much as we love these last few days of warm
weather, it too is a challenge for us. The mornings have
a serious chill factor for the bare toes in our sandals,
but by early afternoon, a tank top is *de rigueur*. None of us
want to see the winter darkness descend again, but it is
time to change the season.

According to Chinese medicine, these two weeks
before the equinox are very difficult for our bodies. It
is a time of exhilaration for new beginnings, after the
full harvest, yet a sadness pervades for the loss of the
bountiful and nurturing growth from our lands.

After the seemingly slow, lazy, warm days, now we must intensify our focus, and get ready for the long, dark days. Many more of us are filling pantries for those days. Given the world chaos, I think it is a return to being unsure, rather than always knowing we could get food here in America. Also, many of us want to return to some nurturing traditions, in order to educate the very young. We are being told to wean them off their "devices," or to limit their use to maybe just one hour a day. I think having them actively involved in the harvest days and pantry preparations is as important for them as getting the spring bulbs in the ground!

Spring bulb ordering already?

Yes, and once again we will order too many, but what a joy over the years to have our collections grow and multiply, and bring all our sweet memories of spring to life again. My absolute favorites are the species crocus and the French tulips. How is that for spring book-ends!

My species crocus are in a pot with a small Japanese maple tree by the front door. The simple green shoots can be seen through the bare branches of the maple. When I first see them, it is almost as exciting as the joyous peeling of the bells in my beloved Rome. With that cold, low light in January or February, when I first spot the small shoots, I then know that warmth and light are indeed returning.

As the days go by, the flowers, very small in comparison with their cousins, such as *Crocus flavus* 'Yellow Mammoth,' stay closed until a ray of sunshine hits them. Then they have no shame, and open their petals to the light. What a fine, sensuous celebration from these demure, little flowers.

I also plant these crocuses in my front garden. Needless to say, when the sun is out, they draw me to my very dormant garden beds. I reconnect with my garden through their vigor. I see all the buds on my deciduous trees fattening. I feel the sense of resurgence in our landscapes. On my walks, I have what one might call "spring-hopeful" eyes.

As for the French tulips, they speak to the abundance of the late April-May garden. The colors are pure French elegance. They stand at least eighteen inches tall. They perform beautifully as cut flowers. Put them in a part of your garden that will receive no summer irrigation; then you can leave them in the ground, year after year.

September 2014

Transition Time

A WEEK OR SO AGO, autumn sent her notice of imminent arrival. She lit up our skies, filled the air with great, booming noises, and then dumped vast quantities of rain onto our parched soils. Yet summer fought back with great fervor, and gave us day after day of sunny warmth, after autumn's short-lived display.

Now, however, the tide has turned and once again, with the great thunderstorm displays last Sunday and cool, cloudy days this week, the transition to our glorious fall season has begun. Have you seen the slight coloration in our deciduous trees? Have you seen the small, but growing, seed heads on our ornamental grasses? Have you seen the minor, yet fetching, greening of our brown lawns?

Perhaps not, for our immediate focus has been on our gardens' tomato glut. Never has there been a tomato harvest in the Northwest to match the one that is ongoing this year. There have been buckets of tomatoes needing to be harvested every day. And yes, we need to transform this bounty into bottled, canned, stewed, sauced, dried, or any other mode of preservation for our winter pantries.

And then there are the beans and the eggplants, not to mention the chard and zucchini, summer squash and peppers. The onions are getting ready for harvesting, along with the potatoes and garlic. Meanwhile, the plums are ripe, but softening, the reddening apples are juicy, and the "experts" are telling us to plant our spring bulbs, plant our winter cover crops, and mulch our soil. Please, just give us some time, and we'll get back to you.

We need to celebrate the bounty. These are the last few days and weeks of the harvest. Harvest time brings our families together, and our broader communities—over grills, at picnics, on patios and decks. Look at the literature and art that have been created around the harvest. We can, and should, carry on the celebratory continuum. And then, when it all gets much quieter, we can plant our spring bulbs and cover crops. We will continue to be with our families and communities, but snug indoors, somewhat away from the bounty of the earth. However, our summer, harvest-created pantries will still be filling our souls and bellies.

September 2013

Autumn

Each day I can recompose the landscape with this season's rich material offerings; it was just a matter of getting past the repetitive chore of the task and finding the craft.

Or, perhaps, the art.

Autumn Light

THE LIGHTING DIRECTORS got it perfectly right last week.

Didn't you find yourself stopping and just basking in the stunningly beautiful autumn light? Sometimes, in the morning, the sun's glare and glint off the fresh dew made me squint. By noon, the night's chill was off the air, yet the light had none of summer's haze. All of our different bodies of water—Elliott Bay below, the water islands in the garden—shimmered in the light, and the sparkle continued into the evening.

Also, we had our first taste of rain. It was such a soft mist, but it was persistent enough to dampen the earth. Then we had the warm-earth damp smells that are startlingly different from irrigated earth smells. There is a chemistry happening in rainwater that I do not understand, but I can smell it. At this time of the year, and again in some spring showers, it has a sweet and delicious fecundity.

Last week we also had the light from a full moon, which made me realize that I am missing Mars. The planet was such an incredible object in our skies last month. It was just there—no need for telescopes. You can still search it out on the distant horizon, fading from our gaze again. There was a great cartoon in *The New Yorker* showing Mars speaking to another planet saying, "Man! That's the closest I've been to Earth in 60,000 years and that's about as close as I ever want to get."

Which reminds us: last week we also lived through the second anniversary of September 11. We do carry on, but the day was a long and uneasy one. I do not think we have yet found our voice about that day two years ago. We continue to struggle with what is fed to us by the media and pundits, or maybe we strive to just push it aside. None of it sits comfortably. Even the benign, temperate climate that surrounds us so gently these first days of autumn leads us to wonder: it looks like paradise, it feels like paradise, yet....

September 2003

There's a Certain Slant of Light

FROM MAY TO SEPTEMBER... That old refrain has been constantly in my head these last few days as I start to clear the garden, in preparation for the autumn leaf drop.

May and September, this year, have turned out to be perfectly matched bookends. Both months were filled with soft, moist days, that at times gave way to hard-driving rains. And nothing in the garden seemed to grow or bloom as expected this summer.

Then, finally, the warm and—might I say?—normal days of September returned this past week. What a joy to be out in the garden wearing short sleeves again. The soil was damp but still warm.

The slight coolness and clear air bring energy after the lazy days and evenings of late summer. And while we all mourn the obvious shortening of the days, the light itself offers its wonderful, autumnal slant on things, illuminating the yellows and reds coming on in greater abundance each day.

This is the time of year to clear out the "old" and bring in the new. Every plant that is transplanted—or newly planted—during the autumn seems to derive a special energy that makes it thrive the following year.

The moist soil, cool nights, dewy morning wetness, and the gentle sun during the day, all contribute to making a spa-like environment for the plants to re-establish themselves.

The lovely autumn light illuminates our careful preparations for winter.

September 1996

Ode to Autumn

OUR AUTUMN DAYS THIS YEAR have been so beautiful one would think they were a gift given in penance for this year's wet summer.

With its beauty, this fall has shown us that the garden is still the place to find considerable enjoyment. The light streams through in soft slants and the clear, warm air of late afternoon gives us the time to plan this season's garden and beyond.

Find the late summer blooming perennials, or the perennials that specifically bloom in this season: the bulbs of autumn, the grasses, and the fall annuals that reach their peak this time of year.

Artemisia, from summer, produce beautiful, gray foliage that can serve as a perfect foil for the intense color of a fall annual, such as *Calliopsis*, or the serenity of the white *Nicotiana*.

My own personal favorite for a fall perennial is the low-growing *Zauschneria californica*, commonly referred to as the hummingbird plant. It produces pure, red tubular flowers, much like a fuchsia, against a quiet, finely-toothed, gray-green foliage. This plant will produce blooms from now until mid-December, at which point it dies back, and is not seen again until July.

It has a very sturdy and slightly invasive root system, which gives it the ability to make a comeback every year. When placing it in your garden, it's important to have nearby a vigorous spring or summer plant that will fill the area left bare until the *Zauschneria* comes once again into leaf and flower.

September 1993

Night Falls Faster

A DREAM CAME TRUE: the warm, sunny weather returned.

I rushed back to the garden Thursday evening filled with plans to continue the projects at hand. Out came the tools and the wheelbarrow as I set to work on this summer's ongoing, wall-building effort.

The light was magnificent as it filtered through the red maple and madrona trees. The air was soft with warmth as I laid out my plans for the evening. I finished up a section of a wall, and started to plant the newly constructed bed. I was enjoying the fruits of my summer labors when I decided to put the tools away and just lazily water the newly placed plants. It seemed luxuriant to back away from the planned projects, but the beauty of the evening caused me to stop and observe with delight my newly designed planting beds.

It turned out to be a good job that I got the tools safely put away, for the night came swiftly, and I could scarcely see what it was that I was watering. No more long, summer evenings. The light disappears ever so quickly these days. There is still much to be done in the garden this season, but one must move fast.

Remember, when you plan your projects, whether they be lawn or perennial bed renewal, or reworking the deck or patio areas, it is important to fashion them in small, manageable increments.

The autumn season has arrived, despite the warmth. It is a busy time in the garden, compressed by the waning light and change in the weather.

October 1994

Color for the Coming Days

OUR FALL DAYS CONTINUE to give us beautiful, warm afternoons in our gardens and glorious colors from our deciduous trees.

While it is true we need to make our spring bulb orders now, there are also wonderful bulbs that should be blooming in our gardens this time of year.

Alliums, which are part of the onion family, can and should be grown outside the vegetable garden. The white flowers of the garlic chive plant (*Allium tuberosum*) create a refreshing, green-white contrast to the red-orange-yellow hues of autumn. Its leaves can be used by the culinary talent in your home, and its flowers add an elegant touch to a mixed bouquet.

With this plant, you will want to bring the flowers inside before they go to seed in your garden, for this plant's only drawback is its alarming talent to propagate from seed.

Other alliums bloom in fall, but their flower colors tend to be in the pink, red, and lavender hues, which may cause some difficulties in a small garden. For a sheer sense of the exotic, there are the cannas, whose popularity peaked in the Victorian age. While they must be lifted and dried for winter, the drama of their foliage, blooms, and seed pods can add a quaint or eccentric accent to an otherwise dull niche.

Most of the autumn crocuses bloom in blue and purple hues, but there is a wonderful, white form, *Crocus ochroleucus*, which blooms in December, adding a spot of brightness to our winter days.

October 1993

Beware of Jarring Effects

I HAVE BEEN REVIEWING the smaller plants of autumn, such as the late-flowering annuals, perennials, and bulbs.

Recently, a wonderful resurgence of interest in ornamental grasses has been occurring, and these plants, in this season, add a remarkable splendor to the garden. They offer a myriad of form and color, while requiring very little maintenance.

The light of this season seems to catch these plants in moments of breathtaking beauty. When the late light of the sun slants through *Imperata cylindrica* 'Rubra,' or Japanese blood grass, "breathtaking beauty" becomes an understatement.

Add to this scene a full planting of *Miscanthus* hybrids in the background, and you will be transported out of the ordinary.

And therein lies one of the problems with this new fashion of the ornamental grasses: they are powerful presences, which can create jarring effects within our traditional Northwest palette. When I see a planting of these grasses in a border, with ferns and rhododendrons within the same view, I feel a great sense of discomfort. I think it's because the symbols of the woodland do not belong right next to those of the savanna in the greater order of things.

October 1993

Autumnal Urgency

BITTERSWEET FEELINGS SWEEP over the avid gardener at this time of year. The dreams of grandeur, of perfection, have been met with the harsh realities of time and weather.

The fullness of summer splendor is now bent and sodden; the harvest is winding down. Yet, with the mere hint of a calm, sunny day, the gardener steps into the garden with wiser eyes. The vigorous growth of a favorite, and perhaps rare, plant gladdens the heart, while the borderline cases are excused for their less-than-stellar performance. The sweetness of these days lies in the hope that the tentative plans for next year will begin to take shape before the year is out.

This can lead to such an invigorating time to be in the garden. The soil is open and moist, the weeds are few and come out with ease. This is an opportunity to make many new plants, by lifting and dividing the perennials, or simply by taking cuttings from the prolific successes, for a vibrant and intense, new focus.

I am surprised by the new crop of weeds, but with a little stirring of the soil with the three-prong cultivator, their days are numbered.

The mind shifts from the disappointments; the temperature is too cool to linger over them. Rather, the crisp, clear, and shorter days of autumn bring an urgency, along with a renewed passion.

October 1997

Yes, Autumn is Here

I THINK THE FALL COLORS are lackluster this year. It is very much like our spring and summer seasons—so many mixed messages from our weather systems.

We try to soldier on with our best intentions, but it is truly remarkable how all is so complex these days. No easy answers seem to pop forth. Just when you think you have recycled everything, and, remembering to bring your own sacks and baskets to the market, you find yourself tearing off another plastic sack for the succulent carrots or juicy tomatoes. I tried this year to use old, flour-sack towels like my mother used in her icebox, but in the rush of the days, I forgot to sprinkle them daily with water. The carrots and lettuce soon went limp. I need to practice more.

And global warming is real. How can we sprint to the point where we reverse its course? I know every little thoughtful bit does help in the long run, as our awareness increases, and the odds for success improve. However, we all have days when it is so tempting to just throw all these new concerns to the wind, get in the car and go for a long drive into the countryside. What carbon footprint?

We need to nurture our sense of place in the garden. In these low-lit days, we need to wonder why we make our gardens—and remember those special times when we planted and schemed and designed with such enthusiasm. The garden does nurture us in such powerful ways. As they say, "my plate was too full today," but with the beautiful sunbreaks in the afternoon, I was fortunate to be able to take the time to just simply be in my garden. It gave so much back to me.

I weeded and clipped and mused, and the hours sped past. I avoided writing this column, and I did not go to the kitchen to cook and transform all the wilting vegetables from last week's CSA box. I stayed in and with the garden. What a fine pleasure on a brilliantly lit Sunday afternoon.

October 2013

Found in the Snowdrop

EVERYWHERE YOU LOOK OR READ, the advice is to buy and plant your spring-flowering bulbs now. However, I find the gigantic and highly colored pictures of the common spring bulbs off-putting.

Spring speaks to me of tenderness and tentative growth—species bulbs can offer a diminutive size to mix in with your plantings.

I combine the yellow *Narcissus* 'Hawera' with the sweet-smelling *Narcissus* 'Thalia' and *Narcissus* 'Actaea.' I mix the common *Muscari armeniacum* with a small sample of full-blown, red tulips. The blue of the *Muscari* softens, yet heightens, the pleasure of the grand, red tulips.

In our climate, it is better to plant the late-flowering tulips such as 'Renown', 'Halcro' or 'Kingsblood'. By using this type, spring storm damage is lessened.

In Paris, forget-me-nots are often underplanted with paired tulips; blue with the red, and pink with the yellow. It makes for a splendid sight in the spring. Of course, a sense of scale is everything. In Paris, we are talking about plantings that use hundreds of bulbs.

Meanwhile, every garden needs the exotic *Fritillaria* bulbs; perhaps not a lot of them, but a taste. And, I cannot imagine a garden without the snowdrops (*Galanthus nivalis*). I see their gray-green shoots come up in January, and can believe that the new year in the garden is ready to burst upon us once again.

It's true that I have to wait, and sometimes for what seems a bottomless amount of time. For courage, in the meanwhile, I contemplate my snowdrops.

October 1995

Welcome to Composting

FALL IS A WONDERFUL TIME to begin a compost pile if you don't have one.

Over the winter the leaves, just by themselves, will produce a rich leaf mold, with no need for action on your part. These leaf piles represent slow, sure ways to compost.

To create greater bulk, simply add kitchen scraps to the leaf pile, stirring them into the decomposing leaves each week. As with all scraps from the kitchen, there should be no meat, fish or chicken bits, and a minimum of grease.

However, coffee grounds are fine, along with eggshells, and even banana peels. If you include the banana peels or other fruit rinds, it helps to dice them into small pieces, for this compost pile of leaves and kitchen scraps is running at a low, even temperature.

Once you include woody stalks, vines, shrub and tree branches in the pile, you need to heat the pile up with nitrogen in order to get the breakdown necessary for the coarser roughage.

So, welcome to composting.

Once you start, the process becomes quite contagious, and you see so many things to add to the pile. It becomes part of your home life, and the process generates an inquisitive nature: how to speed up or slow down the decompression process; when to add accelerators such as nitrogen; when to turn and when to harvest. This is a dynamic process that somehow becomes a compelling part of existence.

The most direct way to compost kitchen scraps is to keep a covered, wet pail in the kitchen, and bury its contents each week in the soil at a depth of eighteen inches. For those of us with no empty garden space to bury these weekly offerings, the worm-box composting technique, known as vermi-composting, is a good, small-scale effort

The set-up is easy, and can be done by mail order. It seems to have a particular charm for children, and the pure gold that it produces needs no sifting. This next step up is the single-bin composter for just kitchen scraps, or a larger receptacle for garden refuse and kitchen scraps.

The array and shapes for this type of composting seems endless and, here again, personal preference comes into play. You will be able to find a bin and its process, along with its accompanying tools, to serve your personal style of composting.

The final step up is the three-pile composting style. These piles can be of any size, and they represent three different stages in the composting cycle.

The first pile takes the current fresh material; the second pile has the start of the decay process, which has been amended and accelerated, and the third pile is the final product. This final product usually needs sifting, so that any parts not fully decayed can be thrown back onto pile two or pile one. Working these piles is like working a bread recipe; they need heat, water, timing, and turning.

All of these composting methods have the same underlying rules and philosophy: the choice, if there is one, is a matter of scale and personal preference. Once you start composting by whatever method, it becomes apparent that our lives and our surrounding landscapes are filled with the raw materials needed for each system.

Once we start composting, a change of perspective comes. We realize our world surrounds us with decay, whether it is in the potholes on our streets, the car not starting when we are late, or the button falling off the last clean shirt.

However, the decay represented in the composting cycles brings the astonishing reward of healthier and more vigorous plants in our garden. And so, the fertility cycle goes on.

October 1994

Dryness Continues

THE BEAUTIFUL FALL COLOR on your deciduous trees may be a sign of drought this year. I found three of my small, newly planted trees seriously suffering from a lack of moisture. Usually, at this time of year, we have had at least a few big rainfalls.

The morning moisture and dew on the paths and plants have deceived me into thinking this is a normal year. But, the big rains have yet to come, and the soil is bone dry.

When I discovered the shriveled leaves, it was necessary to lightly cultivate the soil with a spading fork in order to get the water from my hose to penetrate. Once the trees received a good soaking, the shriveling of the leaves stopped, and I could once again step back and enjoy their fall color.

Everyone is talking about the beauty of this summer's weather. All agree that it was remarkable, and yet, when a soft rain fell one recent Saturday morning, I discovered that everyone I spoke with that day was thrilled with the dampness.

I rushed off to the local bookstore, browsed with pleasure for a long time, came away with a mighty stack of treasures, and entertained pleasurable visions of spending the coming days indoors, with the soft sound of the rain falling outside on the garden.

But not yet. More dry days are predicted. This is a time to keep a close eye on soil dryness, and remove any disparate blooms, in order to help the plants keep up their strength.

October 1994

Time Management

I WAS ASKED THIS WEEK if there was really such a thing as a small, manageable garden project.

I certainly understand what's behind the question. However, it is possible to take charge of the tasks at hand in such a way that portions of the project are accomplished in brief bursts, while the other portions maintain a holding pattern, either for the weather to clear, or for time enough to do the job.

Take, for example, the lifting and dividing of perennials. First, dig up the plants and put them aside. Think about where you might store the clumps for a few weeks. They do not have to be divided immediately; however, they must be kept damp until divided.

Second, dig the soil in the freshly cleared beds, amending it if necessary, but definitely clear the site of any noxious weeds. At the next opportunity, divide the clumps of perennials into small, new plants. These can then be lined out in a flat with soil heaped up on their roots where they can be watered.

Ideally, these small plants will have had their roots cut back to two or three inches in length, and the leaves shorn back to a similar length.

These plants can then stay in the flats for up to four weeks with no harm done. Meanwhile, the renewed planting beds might be sprouting some new weeds, which can easily be removed. Finally, the time will come to replant the new perennials, and to give all your extra new plants to friends or colleagues.

The small, manageable garden project doesn't have to be elusive.

October 1994

The Gift of an Hour

AH, THE BOOKEND IS BACK IN PLACE. Having received the gift of that hour last Sunday, the one so rudely ripped away from us last spring, has brought a feeling of balance to the day again. Sunday morning had the sense of the beginning of a new regime, a new journey, a time to set things right.

First, the appliance manuals had to be located and translated. After a few remarkable and quick successes, the clocks were beginning to fall into place. Isn't it amazing how many different ways have been developed to "set" the time? And then there were the recalcitrant appliances. It did seem that the print and the buttons were surprisingly tiny on these difficult children. Push here, push there, but the results were not forthcoming. Retranslate, try to be courageous, study the fine print to discern where the key instruction had been omitted. And then, finally, not knowing the exact sequence, the desired result was achieved.

The new light in the morning had lulled me into memories and feelings from the summer days, but the loss of light at day's end jolted me into harsh thoughts of the coming winter's cold and darkness. Shaking aside these disquieting musings, I wandered into thoughts about the concept of time. That is a big subject. Starting with the naming done over the centuries, we have Julian calendars, Greenwich Mean Time, which has now been replaced by Coordinated Universal Time, leap seconds, and the faint knowledge that the people in charge of time have to make miniscule adjustments every so often. But I have not found anywhere the naming of the hour that was gifted back to us last Sunday.

October 2003

Frosty Times: Spring in the Murky Depths

LAST SUNDAY, EVEN STANDING with my back to the full sun, I could not erase the deepening chill between my shoulder blades. I tried moving even faster with the garden clean-up chores, but the chill crept under my clothes. Is it already time to wear bulky clothes while working in the garden? The old cliché, "there's frost on the pumpkin," makes this frosty weather sound ever so charming. I, for one, am not ready for such frostiness.

It is still the harvest season. The word "harvest" conjures up warmth. While it is true that the summer squashes now come in baseball-bat sizes, and the tomatoes look luscious, but turn out more often to be mushy inside, we have the beginning of our winter squashes with all their fine markings. And we have heavy pumpkins to lug home, along with sprightly gourds that make our apple piles look a bit surreal.

My sunflower heads are nestled amongst the apple tree branches, with the hopes that the birds will get more than their fair share. Yes, those two types of rats—one with a skinny tail and the other with a fluffy tail—do love to consume the sunflower seeds. It's still a jungle out there.

We have our dreams of perfection; we grab precious hours to fine-tune our dreams; we sometimes look with wonder at all that has happened, and then the autumn cleanup pulls apart and tidies up the chaos. And it takes such a valiant effort. Where did all this vegetative mass come from?

The yard-waste carts advertise our efforts, as the sprawling old squash vines and sturdy sunflower stems poke out the top and sides. Also, we have been told that if you put those green tomatoes in a paper sack, they will ripen. Yes, I did this once. The tomatoes turned red. I sautéed the garlic and onions and added the diced tomatoes. All looked fine. The taste, however, could be described as garlicky cardboard.

So, the frost must be designed to wake us up to the fact that the growing season is ending. The dazzling colors on our deciduous trees brighten our days more than the sun. The cold rains will chase us indoors. But the gardener has a secret for keeping the hope alive. We have been burying bulbs throughout our gardens. Down in those murky depths spring is getting underway.

October 2009

Halloween Thoughts

YECH.

I cleaned out the vegetable garden today. Those tomato plants were scary, with their wilted brown stalks, and waterlogged, squishy green fruit.

Over by the neighbor's wall, his rampant grass and morning glory had made a nested thicket of frightful growth which, when disturbed, brought forth a flurry of creepy-crawly spiders.

It all reminded me of the current Halloween displays, which suddenly seemed tame in comparison. The old stringy spider webs from summer, together with the crinkly, dry, leathery leaves mixed in with the rampant, dried stalks from this season's harvest, must be the source for our spooky Halloween traditions.

The phrase "trick or treat" seems reassuringly correct, if removed from the thought of candy treats.

It is a trick to think that all of our efforts towards growing healthy crops end up in squishy, desiccated forms, yet the fecundity of the wet soil, and the plethora of fat seed pods, are the treats of the season.

We just have to be patient for the return of the light, so that we can start all over again. Meanwhile, while we still have light towards evening, rush out with your pruners when you get home, and make sure the paths and sidewalks are free of any leftover, rampant summer growth.

Aside from wanting to provide safe passage for all those gremlins with their huge shopping bags full of candy, we still appreciate not being hit in the face or rudely brushed on our coats by a drippy, wet branch when the winter dark and damp are upon us.

October 1997

Harbingers of the Season

LAST SATURDAY'S WINDSTORM created a wonderful chaos in the environment. Huge drifts of leaves swirled through the air, and there were times when the leaves came through my open car window as I drove to an appointment.

I spoke with a friend who was working hard in her garden that morning and she felt, as I did, that our lungs had been filled with crisp, raw air. However, when it came time to gather up the leaves and tidy the garden beds, I somehow found other things to do.

I was fortunate to have read this week a brief and wonderful article from a farmer in Nova Scotia, who wrote about his reactions to the harbingers of the various seasons. He wrote about the eagerness he feels to find the first signs of spring, and the dread he feels at the first signs of autumn. There is still so much for him to do, he wrote, and yet when November comes and the fields have their final plowing, a peace finally comes over him. He knows he can turn indoors and rest.

With his writing in mind, I found it less surprising that I had little heart for the raking and tidying of the garden. It is indeed time to rest and be indoors, planning our first holiday harvest with our families, friends, and community.

October 1993

Combinations to Consider

BEFORE THE LAST of the autumn color blows away, here are some plant combinations to think about.

The European mountain ash (*Sorbus aucuparia*) is a tree with delicate, fern-like foliage that has a splendid color range, incorporating all the yellows, oranges, and reds of the season. The small fruit, which appears in mid-summer, adds the orange-red color; these berries often stay on the tree winterlong.

It's easy to grow, and has not become more popular due to a perceived messiness from the dropping berries. Planted in combination with western red cedars (*Thuja plicata*), or other plants in the *arborvitae* family, they provide a colorful divergence from the ubiquitous maple trees.

The sourwood tree (*Oxydendrum arboreum*) offers a brilliant, scarlet color to the autumn landscape, along with mid-summer clusters of its white, bell-shaped flowers. Planted with the strawberry tree (*Arbutus unedo*), all of its horticultural requirements can be met.

The sourwood rarely answers to the description of an elegantly shaped tree, and its roots need to be in the shade with its crown in the sun. However, nestled between the dark, shiny leaves of the strawberry tree, which also produces bell-shaped flowers, the combination can be very handsome.

Both of the plants in this combination are considered to be slow-growing types; perhaps this is why they are rarely seen in general cultivation. This concept of "slow-growing" has kept many plants from being used more widely. Don't be fooled by the concept. My experience has shown that they all come along very nicely, and offer any number of desirable touches to the garden.

November 1994

The Art of Raking

AS WITH ALL ART FORMS, your choice of tools is paramount.

Springier tines in a rake offer greater flexibility, and help to relieve the impact on your body. Ironically, the inexpensive, old-fashioned bamboo rake comes closer to the ideal than the seen-everywhere, inexpensive, plastic, immovable rake.

It breaks my heart when I see these plastic rakes being used; they transmit all of the raking impacts back onto the body, and they're incapable of doing corners, where the wind usually deposits most of the leaves.

Having procured a fine tool, the challenge then comes to find an approach to the task at hand that will keep the spirit alive, and away, from those mundane thoughts that arise when we regard raking as a tiresome, repetitive chore.

I think of a phrase from one of Van Gogh's letters to his brother in 1889, noting: "...the various effects of a gray sky against a yellow soil, with a green-black note in the foliage; another time the soil and the foliage are all of a violet hue against a yellow sky; then again a red-ocher soil and a pinkish-green sky."

It is the range of colors, both in the leaves and the atmosphere, which can bring immense enjoyment. As does the arrangement of the leaves.

After getting the bulk of them from the edges, the corners, and the garden beds, the pleasure comes in deciding how many to leave behind and where to leave them. The other day I felt like I was composing a landscape painting while making these decisions.

I knew I would have more materials offered to me the next day, so where, today, did I want to paint the earth? Each day I can recompose the landscape with this season's rich material offerings; it was just a matter of getting past the repetitive chore of the task, and finding the craft.

Or, perhaps, the art.

November 1994

Late Autumn in the Garden

THE RACE IS ON.

Eagerly we have stocked up on bulbs from our local garden emporiums, and for those rare treasures seldom found in retail outlets, our fingers have pushed (far too many times) the "add to shopping cart" button on the wide, wonderful, world of the internet.

Many packages have arrived on our doorsteps this week, and we have decided, for these magical springtime bulbs, that we simply will not calculate a carbon footprint. The time has come to slip all these treasures into our dreams about the spring landscape.

Getting the bulbs ready and into an easy receptacle to carry out to the garden takes a bit of time. There is the fuss of removing the papery excess, and then remembering to note in the frayed garden journal just exactly where the treasures are to be buried. Where did that half-hour go? And then preparing the garden beds requires a little(?) bit of cleaning out of both the old pine needles, the fresh fallen, and the oh-so colorful autumn leaves.

Aha, now to dig in those bulbs. Except it would make sense to move that fern—which is blocking the pleasure of seeing the growth of that small, rare azalea—and it makes sense to fill in that space with those coral bells that need to be divided—the ones in the crowded bed over by the (fill in the blank).

The instructions that come with most bulbs always advise that you add some rich bulb food as you plant the bulbs. Am I going to sprinkle into each bulb hole a dollop of plant food? Actually, no. It is all that I can do to try to get just one accursed bulb at the proper and advised level. And I bought one-hundred of these?

Now the smarter garden makers have decided to have their spring bulb displays in pots. While I struggle to get the bulbs into my garden beds, they just simply line up their gorgeous and extensive garden pot collections, add fresh potting soil, and lay out the bulbs. It is possible to plant a pot with tulips at the greatest depth, followed by daffodils, and then some wonderful crocuses on the final layer. Dress it all off with handsome potting soil, water thoroughly, keep damp through the winter months, and *voila*, a gorgeous spring display.

However, my not so quiet 'tsk-tsk' comes when they all say, "Well, of course I get fresh bulbs every year." I say this is not gardening, this is window dressing. But then there is an enchanting beauty, in the spring, with their beautifully articulated arrangements. I look out at my garden beds, hoping to see my bulbs emerge— and they do, but never as thoroughly or dramatically as my brilliant gardening friends' potted spring displays.

I admire their drama. Then I console myself, as the light gets longer and stronger, with the hardiness and beauty of the bulbs I planted when the light was waning.

Of course, I want the best of all worlds, yet I have not been able to make my own collection of spring bulb containers. I continue to leave that to the *artistes*—for I need to concentrate on getting all the bulbs planted before November 16. Yes, it is a totally arbitrary date, but from past experience, it is a totally necessary date. There have been years when I have found paper sacks filled with bulbs, dry and empty as dust.

The days of late autumn flew past, and those bulbs did not get planted.

November 2007

The Wonders of the November Garden

PLANT YOUR BULBS. Plant your bulbs. Plant your bulbs.

So goes the mantra.

In fact, I've planted bulbs in January and they have been quite fine.

There is much to be done, but the first priority is to look out, and find ways to care for the public landscape attached to our homes. Are the sidewalks covered in slippery leaves, or are the gutters full with the potential to impact the local storm drain? I find that many people, passing where I rake and tend the public landscape, find my efforts laudable, but quixotic. Today I talked with a dedicated community-oriented soul, who was tending the sidewalks and gutters near her home. She told me that most people, including the real estate woman who sold her their home, find her work quite strange. Why, said the real estate woman, would you want to muck about with this stuff on the street?

If you have to ask the question, then there is no hope for understanding. A dear friend, who is getting on to being elderly, has now had to find different routes for his daily walk, because of his favorite sidewalks' excessive, slippery detritus. Next week I might walk with him, carrying my favorite Flexrake, and clear the sidewalks for him. They are public, after all. Will I be bringing shame to the home owners? That is not my intent. Rather I would hope for insight and understanding, and the opportunity for digging deeper into sharing and celebrating our community.

It is a time when the "interactive" hours in our gardens are significantly shortened. If you cannot work from home, then you leave for, and return from, your job when it is dark, and on your days off the weather might be so perfectly foul that you are not drawn out into your garden. Once you do get out to the garden, the sheer joy of observation takes over, and all the want-to-do jobs get not-done.

A crow landed on the roof of my garage with a big biscuit of some sort in his beak. He jumped down into the gutter. Oh, I thought, a bit of rain-water softening is in order. No, he pulled up a wad of gutter detritus to cover his cache, and he was off for more from his source. Squirrels have been hiding their treasures. Small birds are filling the trees and their stomachs with seeds, showing almost no fear from any activity on the ground.

And then, recently, there was my special flicker, taking a bath in one of my water pots. His hen was with him. They danced around the edge of the pot, each splashing in the water. Then the hen flew away, and he went wild, jumping in and out of the pot, ruffling his feathers with such abandon, and then flew to the garage roof, where he preened with the sunshine on his back. Then the hen returned, and had some very sweet, demure baths by herself. I think it may have been their first "date night" since the kids had flown their nest.

With the weak light now, and the chill inundating our hands, neck, and great behinds as we bend over to clear and prune and plant, the time for inspiring observation has been severely shortened. I stare at my trees and shrubs that need pruning (later in the year), and the bulbs don't get planted, the treasures from my summer plant-hunting at the nurseries don't get potted up or installed in the current design, and the clearing and winter mulching do not proceed. When I refocus away from such pleasurable observing, I rush through the projects, just hoping that all their aspects and issues will be able to survive my lack of total concentration.

November 2012

Daphne bholua

CURRENTLY, THE EVERGREEN, winter-flowering shrub, *Daphne bholua*, is showing off its full-blown, blooming splendor. And even with the cold temperatures, its fragrance is noticeable many feet away. The scent is slightly musky, which leads to thoughts of warm and pleasantly humid temperatures. Then a gust of wind slaps your cheek, ending those brief daydreams. Regrettably, the plant does not do well as a cut flower. The scent soon disappears, the small flowers wither, and the leaves get droopy, all within a few hours of bringing the branches, covered with blooms, indoors.

This daphne is native to the eastern Himalayas. Over the years, many cultivars have been developed by breeders, the most popular one being 'Jacqueline

Postill'. Whichever cultivar you choose, the plant will grow as an open and upright shrub with lance-shaped, medium, dark-green leaves. The small, pink-purple, waxy buds open to reveal white, fragrant flowers. The slight variation to the blooms amongst the cultivars is lost on me.

Once established, daphne plants can rarely be successfully transplanted.

Additionally, they do not take kindly to heavy pruning. Like many winter and spring-flowering plants, the time to do any pruning is when the plant is in flower. And that is why it is such a disappointment that the pruned branches cannot make spectacular, indoor flower arrangements. It is possible, however, to make small noisette arrangements of the flowers, with the stems cut to within three to four inches of the blooms. These little cuttings can remain fresh-looking for a few days.

Ideally, the plant should be situated within an eastern, northeastern or northwestern site, with plenty of light and not too much direct sun. My wildly successful shrub (envied by some dear friends) obviously landed in the right northeastern spot. It is nestled within a grove of *Stewartia monadelpha* trees, so it gets plenty of light during the late fall and winter seasons. Then it receives filtered sunlight during the spring and summer seasons.

The soil is very sandy, and only receives modest irrigation during late July, August, and early September. There is a thick layer of coarse mulch and *Heuchera micrantha* plants nestled around the base of the shrub. The shrub does not possess a particularly strong structural shape, so for me its beauty is the glory of its winter-flower display. As the stewartia trees start to leaf out in the spring, the not-very-distinctive shrub melts away into the background. It is next to the path that I use to haul out all those waste and recycling cans. So, even with the winter winds blowing, and the cold rain pelting, I at least interact with its winter glory on a weekly basis.

November 2008

Soup Time

THIS EARLY COLD SPELL seems to fit in with all the anomalies occurring these days, including the tragic scale of the Southern California fires. On the whole, weather and politics run amok.

I am playing with fire (ice, actually) by not shutting off the watering systems out in the garden, but it is much too early. This is the season to plant, to transplant, to make the garden right for next year. Please, the big chill from the north needs to back off.

Sunday's snow, mixed with rain, did drive me back to my favorite January recipes. I was looking for the ones that did not require soaking the beans overnight—I wasn't that well prepared. However, I longed for a truly hearty winter meal. And then I stumbled upon one of my most favorite and simple soups. It can easily be adjusted to include any of your preferred ingredients. It is a classic:

½ cup each of chopped onions, chopped celery, and tomato sauce

1 garlic clove, chopped

1 cup washed lentils

8 cups hot water or light broth

¾ cup arborio rice

Sauté the onions and celery in olive oil, add the garlic, and cook for a minute or two. Add the lentils, tomato sauce, and water. Simmer for about thirty-five minutes, or until the lentils are almost cooked. Add the rice, and cook gently for twenty minutes, checking it often, just as you would with risotto, so that it doesn't become sticky or too thick. Add water if needed. Most importantly, let the soup rest for five minutes when you determine that the rice is cooked. Then garnish it with chopped cilantro, or parsley, or whatever taste treat amuses you. Salt and pepper to taste, and top with some grated Pecorino Romano cheese. A glass of wine, a big piece of fresh warm bread, and the biting cold air has evaporated.

November 2003

Early Brrrrr, But So Beautiful ...

I HOPE YOU SAW the glorious new rim of white surrounding the Puget Sound Basin today, before the clouds came in low again. Sunday, the Olympic Mountains were lit up by the early morning sun. Stopped you in your tracks. Such brilliance was startling after so much gray.

It made you realize that the recent bareness of the mountains was all wrong for this region. Now, the basin has refreshed its ephemeral qualities: white mountain peaks, reflected up close in whitecaps on the waters. And then the clouds drift back in, mists obscure the brilliant clarity, and you wait again for the next grand showing.

Meanwhile, there is all this colorful, sodden confetti on the ground. Raking the leaves is much harder work than the romantic image of huge leaf piles, with little children gleefully throwing themselves into the piles.

As for the rest of the garden, it is now just a mad scramble to get the bulbs planted, and to clean up the wilted summer glory. And it doesn't help to have incessant, heavy rain occurring on the weekend days. I look at my rain gear, and I really just want to leave it in the closet. Am I becoming a fair-weather gardener? I do find that I am beginning to be highly envious of those gardeners in other regions, whose gardens get shut down for them by a fresh blanket of snow. For them, there is no room for procrastination.

So, here is the perfect scenario: a sunny, but not too-warm weekend. All the eager skiers can leave for the slopes and celebrate this year's amazingly early season. The gardeners in the house can luxuriate in long, extended hours of puttering and straightening, pruning and bulb planting. On the back burners of the stove will be huge pots of stews and soups, quietly burbling their way towards perfection. And then late Sunday evening, a gathering at the table for hearty fare, and a long round of chatter about whose sore muscles get to be soaked in the tub first.

November 2005

Crisp to Sodden

THE WIND WHIPPED UP A HUGE flurry of orange, red, yellow, and brown leaves last week, causing a genuine sense of chaos on our streets and sidewalks. Driving or walking through this highly colorful scene was disorienting, for the ground had lost its distinct form. All seemed the same, whether at ground level or up to the treetops and beyond.

Images of the funhouse, or a scary, disorienting movie, or going down the rabbit hole into a changed reality came to mind. And the brisk air and bright sunshine made it feel all so invigorating.

There are these few weeks when our surrounding landscapes dazzle us with their colors and chaos. We continue to have spots of orange roundness staring quietly at us, as the pumpkins and gourds slowly slump, or list softly to one side. For a brief moment, the sun will shine between showers, illuminating the dark, wet bark, and the shimmering drops of water clinging to the leaves. This is magical stuff when we take the time to stop and marvel.

Then the rains continue, softening the brittle edges, and finally turning the disquieting frenzy into a mushy pulp. Raking the sidewalks and the gutters helps to set things right, to bring a sense of clarity. I am always amazed at how fast the squiggly little worms arrive to feast on the wet leaves. Where do they hang out until their banquet arrives?

Pulling the composting leaves off the lawn, out of the ground-cover plantings, or out of the corners where the wind has stacked them high, is tedious, soggy work.

During this tedium, thoughts of the forest floor come to mind. Why don't we design our landscapes so they can function like a forest, quietly absorbing all this colorful leaf matter, and letting the process of winter's weather turn it into soil? The branch snags could be used for making a fire crackle. And the warmth and woodsy smells from that fire would remove the dank chill that seeps in from the outside.

November 2003

It Warms the Blood

I OFTEN HEAR HOW LUCKY we are to be able to garden year-round on the West Coast.

And of course, it's true.

However, gardening in these cool days is a far cry from the blissful warmth of the late spring, summer, and early fall days. One must move with speed and fortitude now, in order to keep the chill, moist air from penetrating our wet gloves and damp shoes.

And yes, we are fortunate to have a plethora of deciduous trees dropping their leaves all over these days. A brisk raking up of the latest droppings gets the blood moving and warmed, so that we can then go back to lifting and dividing the perennials, and the other quietly rewarding jobs in our garden.

The other blood-warming activity involves cleaning out the garage, in order to find room to store the hoses and pots. This latest chilly weather reminded us all that it is time to turn off the water, drain and store the hoses, and empty the water gardens and fountains. It's also the time to bring indoors the tender plants, and to clean up and secure special pots from winter freezes.

But we don't have to lay down special mulches to protect our roses, nor do we have to provide winter protection for our robust perennials. We do, however, need to check where, and how, all the rainwater is moving through our landscapes, and to make sure that either erosion or standing water areas are dealt with.

Keep the water moving away from your home, and mulch heavily for erosion protection. And then look up and savor the autumnal light, illuminating the rich, seasonal colors with its slanting rays.

November 1996

Somebody Get Me to a Woodpile

ALMOST ALL OF THE AUTUMNAL elements are in place: the electrifying bright and cold sunshine; the fiery blazes of color on the deciduous trees; winds sweeping that color into the landscape and finally into the darkened, moist ground.

Hats, gloves, and layers of clothing to ward off the morning chill must be put on in the weak light of morning, but still hope lingers that the afternoon sun will provide the warmth to shed those layers. And our schedules have lost their summertime pace, for the light is seriously waning, and we find ourselves unable to linger late into the evenings, as we did with the summer light.

The one element of the season that seems to have disappeared from our lives is the ritual of creating the woodpile for winter. You probably remember a time when there was a mound of split logs, or even just a collection of logs that needed to be split and formed into a sturdy woodpile. We were all told that the woodpile warmed you three times—first with the act of collecting the wood, then the splitting, and finally the burning.

The actual stacking or creation of the woodpile does not count in the warming equation, for the skill required is not a physical activity, but rather has a timelessness that speaks to the intellect, and to that unspoken knowledge of form. In other words, the same qualities needed to make a stone wall.

Construction of the woodpile requires a clear focus. Just as in a wall, the foundation will define the beauty of all successive efforts.

At first, it seems that every piece one picks up is hopelessly wrong for the job; too small, too uneven, too bulky. However, with perseverance, the right pieces start to make themselves known, and a definite rhythm comes into play. Your hands and eyes seem to find the right piece for the right place, and the mind finally gets to wander with thoughts about where the wood came from, and how it grew to such form. A great sense of excitement grows along with the emerging woodpile. The beauty of form emerges, when you have done it right.

November 1994

The Why of Trees

THE COLD, CLEAR, and brittle air with pink mornings and pink evenings has produced a truly remarkable, autumn-colored spectacle this year.

But now the winds have returned, disturbing the chilled silence and leaving the colors of autumn blown all over the place. So why, we might ask ourselves as we reach for the rake, do we plant all this deciduous bother?

Because, we might answer, planting a tree, or multiple trees, renews our hopes for the generations that come after us. As we grow old, we watch the trees grow in stature. Watching them, we might forget life's "fever and the fret," as Keats put it. In them, we see growth and renewal, year by year. In addition to providing shade and shelter from the rain, they stand tall against life's imponderables. We can touch them, smell their sweet blooms, or marvel at their winged seeds. And maybe we can plant a new one each season.

November 1994

Helping Hands for the Holidays?

COLD AND WET SOIL, light but crisp, chill winds, and miniscule hours of light, greet us in the garden this season.

So, it is necessary to move swiftly and with purpose when the weather allows, to finish this year's garden projects, and to prepare the garden for next year's dreams.

Remember, you are not alone as you take necessary shortcuts. The digging of great holes, and the dumping of this year's bulbs into those holes with no amendments or extra care, is the modus operandi of all great gardeners caught by the chill of approaching winter.

The wet soil makes transplanting projects a piece of cake. The shovel easily enters the soil, and at least I do not feel like a killer if I chop off some of the root mass. The dampness feels so fecund; though I could be proved wrong, I believe the moisture and cold help the plant to rest and grow slowly and well.

Soon, we will all be busy indoors with holiday preparations. Take advantage of the extra helping hands gathered around the hearth at year's end. Let them help in the garden.

Make it a fun place to escape from football on TV, or debates over changes made to family recipes. Small hands are especially adept at getting the last of the autumn leaves out of the shrubbery, and most everyone likes to impose their sense of orderliness, whether it be the woodpile or how cleaned pots and tools are stored. 'Tis the season, we're told, for giving and sharing. Sometimes those virtues rise up in unexpected ways.

November 1994

It's the Weather

THE FOG IS PERSISTENTLY present and thick. Around here, that means it is the long Thanksgiving weekend. And we will all be looking for our friends and relatives somewhere out there in the mist and fog of revised arrival times.

To add to the chaos, there is a cold storm due to arrive during the week, after the long holiday weekend.

This will be the first real challenge in many years for gardeners who fell in love with exotic and tender tropical plants. The forecasters are predicting twenty degree weather, so those plants will need much wrapping and bundling to survive outdoors.

Then there is the ritual of turning off the outside water sources, emptying and turning over the water pots, draining the hoses, cutting back the dying peony foliage to expose the new, fat buds so they don't rot, and finding snow boots, mittens, and hats. When will I find the time to perfect that exotic, new recipe I promised for the Thanksgiving table?

Or, I could wait to shut down the garden until the day after Thanksgiving, and by scheduling it that way, I would also avoid the shopping rush. It is known in the retail trade as Black Friday, and all the merchants who rely on it for their yearly success are ready to tempt you greatly on that day. It is fun to go out and to be mobbed and to complain about it all. Especially if you have had serious discussions about not being caught up in the shopping frenzy of the season. Secretly, we all know that we find great pleasure in it. It just seems unseemly if the pleasure is not masked by outrageous complaining.

I regret the cynicism, but so much of our culture is involved with skirting around these issues. We bemoan the commercialization of the holiday season, yet we partake. We scramble to find some personal meaning, but often run out of time. When the snow flies next week, despite the inconveniences, maybe we'll sit quietly for a few moments, and watch the swirling flakes with a renewed sense of wonder and delight. Then hold tight to those sweet feelings.

November 2005

Even Now Our Gardens Still Need Us

"PUREED, THE ROOT VEGETABLES of late fall and early winter are a soothing, sturdy panacea for the chilly emptiness brought on by wet winds and fallen leaves."

These words by Molly O'Neill, writing in the *New York Times Magazine*, could also be used to describe our gardens and their holiday decorations. By cleaning up the last of the fallen leaves, and tidying and mulching our flower beds, we can bring a soothing order to our winter gardens.

With the addition of lights and garden holiday decorations, our gardens can once again bring fulfillment to us as we prepare our year-end festivities. One approach is to use branches from your pruning work to create an interesting structure in the garden, which can hold lights, or hand-made snowflakes, or ribbon-tied bunches of herbs, such as lavender and rosemary.

Of course, cut boughs from evergreens are perfect for decorating our entryways. Add herbs, grasses, and berries for a more complex arrangement.

The attention paid to the garden now will lift our spirits when the winds howl and the rain drums our window panes. Though this is the busy indoor season, our gardens still need our mindful care.

December 1993

The color of springtime is in the flowers. The color of winter is in the imagination.

—Ward Elliot

Holiday Season Beginnings

SUDDENLY, THE LIGHTS are appearing again: the roof structures outlined, the tree branches lit up, the dripping cascades of light dancing in the breeze.

This season of lights has just begun. I find the job entirely too laborious, and therefore have great admiration for those who have the patience to make the installations. How do they do it? I have tried, and only ended up with a mass of kink, which I then lob at the structure and tell myself that it is art.

I do put lights on the indoor Christmas tree, but as the years speed by the tree becomes smaller and smaller. This requires less winding around and under, and a lot less cursing. Perhaps I will hire one of our local artisans, who obviously can trim beautiful and fully-recognized structures with lights. Then I could fill a big tree with all of my favored ornaments.

If you stay quiet, and reflect upon the nature of what we are doing this season, it becomes clear that we are making light to fill the darkness. The sun is way far south, but will be returning to our hemisphere later this month. Meanwhile, we have created rituals to light our paths during this darkness. We need to have the darkness filled with music, and that has been done with the special tunes, hymns, and other "traditional" music within the world religions and folk cultures. We need to have the darkness filled with stories that reflect the mysteries of darkness, but also lead us towards hope.

December 2003

Winter Gardening

TOO COLD AND SO SOON—the fiery colors of autumn so swiftly gone.

Just a few days ago, we were all complaining about the rain and wind and all the sodden leaves to rake up. Of course, some of us would dearly love to have some gentle rains to soften our brittle landscapes. Of course, others want snow. Either scenario simply informs us that it is wintertime in our gardens. And many would suggest that the winter garden is the best garden, for our garden work consists of dreaming the perfect garden!

The first catalogs are arriving, tempting us to spend hours pouring over the glorious pictures and descriptions and making lists. If one were to study the lists carefully, our gardens would be an acre or two in size.

If you are new to gardening or this region, make sure you get to know the Territorial Seed catalogue (TerritorialSeed.com). All of their products have been tested for geographic appropriateness. This can really help the novice gardener.

Another fine resource is the Seed Savers Exchange (seedsavers.org). This organization was founded in 1975 with a mission to "save the world's diverse but endangered garden heritage for future generations by collecting, growing and distributing heirloom seeds."

If you join the Exchange, you will have access to thousands of rare seeds, and a quarterly magazine filled with information about the work of people around the world working on the issues of food and nutrition systems.

While hours can fly by reading and doing research on the internet, a good book still brings such greater pleasure. Snuggling into a chair and entering another world happens with books. During my very brief strolls out in the winter garden, I find myself looking for those first tentative bulb shoots. For sheer enjoyment, I hurry back to my chair and Anna Pavord's book, *Bulb*.

The book is an amazing production. Six hundred bulbs are discussed, with a photograph for each one. While seemingly encyclopedic, it does not cover the entire range of bulbs, corms, tubers, and rhizomes. Rather, this is a very personal account, along with the standard information on hardiness, bloom times, height, and planting tips. Some might argue that she is too opinionated. For example: "In the lilies listed below you will not find any of the new dwarfed kinds, which I think are foul—lacking in any of the grace and elegance with which nature endowed the family."

I find her insights to be amusing and thought-provoking.

December 2009

Garden Gifts: Be Very Clear

THE SPLENDOR OF SPRING will eventually return to us; now is a good time to think about what tools, plants, or garden artifacts would bring the most pleasure to our days spent in the garden.

Would a new, commercial-grade garden hose bring relief from the knotted, old, tired, duct-taped Hydra which last year knocked the blooms off your favorite delphinium? Is this the year to find an early, winter-blooming camellia to be planted where you can easily enjoy its tender promise of the gardening glories ahead?

What about a gift certificate from your favorite nursery? Just thinking about all the different possibilities for spending it constitutes an indoor sport these short days.

Will this be the year to change to a push mower for the sake of exercise, quietness, and better lawn health? Or will most of the lawn be removed in order to install a kitchen garden, a rose garden, or a rhododendron dell?

Our gardens contain so many elements and dimensions that it's good policy to be very clear to those who ask what sort of gift would most please us. And it is important to give to others the gardening gifts that speak to their particular garden joy. And finally, the gift of a seed or a plant perfectly expresses the celebration of life, which is the motif underlying all of our holiday celebrations.

December 1993

Solstice: Prepare to Pivot

WILL THERE BE A PERCEPTIBLE CHANGE in our gardens after next Saturday's winter solstice?

Since the fullness of summer, we have been watching the withering away, the stripping bare, the loss of abundance. On Saturday, the process is reversed: the long march toward fullness resumes. The sun, having bumped up against its farthest reach to the south, turns north. At least that's how we see it from earth, though the earth is the one actually doing the turning.

Throughout the myriad of cultures past and present, humans have performed deep rituals to celebrate the return of the light. The candles people have been lighting since the autumn equinox are to keep the darkness at bay. Now we prepare to light the candles in honor of the light's return.

Soon, green pointy tips from the bulbs we buried on those cool autumn days will part the winter soil. The snowdrops (*Galanthus nivalis*), will bloom even as they're drummed by icy winter winds. The bright blooms of the forsythia will shine like yellow torches out of the gray winter landscape. The early cherry tree blossoms portend the coming days when our cold winds and rain are behind us.

These welcome auguries await fulfillment. In the meantime, first comes the pivot. And rebirth of light.

December 1996

Winter

I stand up and am caught by surprise at the length of my shadow in front of me, and then I remember it is still winter, in spite of the sun's warmth.

The Returning Light

HALLELUJAH! It will not get any darker. And those endless "H" choruses resonate so fully within me. One can see the celebration of the newborn as a powerful and moving symbol for the return of the light.

We look on our cold, dank gardens as spiritless places, yet upon closer inspection, buds are fattening, and bulb shoots tell us that regeneration is happening beneath the surface. When the temperatures soften into the fifties, long slimy earthworms, if disturbed in the leaf litter, ooze about and become targets for our few remaining birds. Except for the crows and the gulls, the birdsong is quiet.

The winter solstice is a defining moment, best remembered when the chilling January winds come, not to mention the insults of March. The light does return ever so slowly; it is, in fact, in an upward arc.

All of our neighbors who have lit their homes and landscapes deserve our salutations. The darkness can be so pervasive, but their work brings a much- needed light, and sweet joyousness, to our communities. While waiting for greater, fuller sunlight, our decorative lighting festivities help to counter the darkness of the season.

We bake and roast and slow cook—all nestling and nurturing. We also reach out with coats and gloves and hats and food and shelter to others whose lives are compromised. It is a season of giving, of being aware that as humans there is a deep-seated need to embrace, to reach out.

As our gardens slowly unfold their new blossoms and spring growth, we try to remember the promises made to family and friends at this time of the year. We really did mean what we said about helping them with the garden chores. It is such a lovely gift—the gift of time.

December 2009

My Tree of Hope

A TIME TO PAUSE in the winter garden and reflect on the past year's wonders and delights.

I remember the chaos, noise, and filth when the gas company arrived on my street this summer, bringing with them no-parking signs, numerous big trucks, and loud equipment. I talked with the crews about my young street trees and how important they had become to the neighborhood. While it was true that the leaves on one of eight trees had turned a deep bronze color in the spring, and showed no signs of growing into a mature tree, it hadn't died completely, either. I asked that the crew be careful of it, as much as the surrounding trees.

The sheer joy, delight, wonder and enchantment came a few days later when they had found, and fixed, a leak in the gas main in the street close to the impaired tree's roots.

I set a sprinkler and gave it a luxurious, two-hour bath in the warmth of the evening. Ten days later, all of its leaves were green again. It is growing beautifully and now has become, and will always be, my tree of hope.

The tree's startling transformation has caused me to think a lot about the strength of plants. It seems they do carry on in the worst of conditions at times, not stopping or waiting to be helped by the gardener's hand.

I have come to be amused by the guile and health of the weeds that nestle next to, and around, the permanent plants. I watch with admiration as all the plants bend and twist to reach for the light. All this strength and motion is at rest in the winter garden. For now.

December 1994

The New Year with Our Dream Plants

THE THIN, GRAY LIGHT this month creates quiet scenes out our windows, while indoors we surround ourselves with full-color plant catalogues and lengthy order lists. Leafing through these seductive tomes, the mind wanders and then leaps into flights of fancy. Must have this, and this, and …

How quickly we forget the treasures already existing in our gardens.

Pulling on some warm, bulky clothes, I took a fast amble through my winter-chilled garden on New Year's Day. There were new, luminescent blobs close to the ground that will soon unfurl into hellebore flowers. The *Daphne bholua* was covered with small, soft-pink florets. The buds of the Japanese spicebush, *Lindera obtusiloba*, were deliciously fat, just waiting to burst open in the next few days. The species crocus greens were up through the mulch layer, and the winter irises, *Iris unguicularis*, were unfurling their blooms. These first irises of the season, I think, put the later blooming *Iris reticulata* to shame. The markings are more complex, and the exquisite fragility of the blooms belie the harsh chill in the air. And, of course, the *Camellia*

174

sasanqua 'Setsugekka' was stunningly covered with its pure, white blooms.

Returning to my piles of catalogs, I found it much easier to start editing the order lists. If I have this much blooming in the wee light of January, do I want a huge thicket of blooms later in the year? Do I need to have all that new, newer, newest? Well, yes, some of them.

Then I started to read the plant descriptions with a great deal more care. I have gardened long enough to be wary of phrases like "vigorous, spreading clumps." Three years after the initial planting those clumps have become thugs in the garden. You know you need to lift and divide them, but you stall for one more year, and so the "thuggishness" also greatly increases. Finally comes the day with the spading fork, and you know you have to root it all out, and you think twice about passing on this once new, newer, newest plant to a friend.

January 2006

Starting Anew

HAPPY NEW YEAR GREETINGS to all, including the Comcast trucks that continue to garishly prune my street trees with their bucket operations.

It seems early this year, but the snowdrops, *Galanthus* (*Amaryllidaceae* family), are already throwing out their delicately sturdy blooms. I checked my yearly diaries, and actually it is not too early for them to be strutting their stuff. The difference this year must be that I planted a lot of them in one of my garden beds by the front door. In previous years, they had been located way down the hill, under some dripping wet conifers. Not a site often visited during these low-lit days.

Snowdrops create fine, fat clumps, or drifts, after a few years in the ground. To expand your drifts of this early bloomer, you can lift and replant the bulblets elsewhere, just as their foliage is about to wither later in the spring. Some experts feel that you need to lift and divide these clumps every three years. This non-expert finds that not to be the case—the blooms here continue to be exuberant in volume and height. And they seem to thrive in sun and shade. However, they do not do well with summer drought, unlike the *Iris unguicularis,* another early winter bloomer, which only does well with dry summer conditions.

Woodland gardens in the United Kingdom are famous for their fine drifts of snowdrops. However, in our more modest gardens, if we drifted the snowdrops to that scale, we would have no room for our beloved daffodils, tulips, early spring irises, and crocuses. In addition, snowdrops do not look well as single specimens. So, a compromise is in order here, with a bit of clumping and drifting that celebrates their sweet demureness.

Since the 1990s, there has been an incredible resurgence of snowdrop breeding. The name comes from the Greek *gala* (milk), combined with *anthos* (flower). There are only eighteen species, but from that stock it is now possible to have over 150 varieties.

Their differences mostly elude my sensibilities. I have seen the doubles, and I have studied some varieties with incredibly beautiful markings, but when seen out in the chilly winter garden, the unique characteristics do not bring me to my knees in celebration. I do offer my sincerest apologies to the snowdrop collectors and hybridizers. Their work is fascinating, their patience is inspiring.

Trees, shrubs, perennials, and annuals go through fashion periods. Much of this change can be related to media experts singing the praises of a long-forgotten favorite, and to different horticultural practices.

As we move into the teen decade of the twenty-first century, we are seeing yet another huge change in fashion. For many people, the exquisitely planned and carefully tended perennial border, such an avant-garde fashion statement at the turn of the century, has become much less interesting. The thrill is gone, and the labor-intensive aspects no longer hold much appeal. The semi-hardy tropical look also lost its compelling allure after the deep-freezing devastation of 2008. As well, there is the boredom of these plants, which arises because they offer a one, or at most two-dimensional, seasonal interest to the overall garden scheme.

Fashion has now moved on to make us beholden to creating the ultimate vegetable garden. Sounds delicious to me, and I dream about that smell from the leaves of the tomato plants, not to mention the dreams of fresh pesto—summer incarnate, along with our towering sunflowers. But as we move into this New Year, let us not forget to sing the praises of the first snowdrop, and the cheerful, neon-brightness of a daffodil on a Northwest-gray, blustery day.

January 2010

Dreams for the New Year

IN THESE EARLY COLD, gray-lit days of the New Year, all dreams are possible for our gardens. Perfection and beauty will reign supreme. The winds will always be tempered, the few freezes will be short-lived, the rains will not pelt down late in spring, the summer heat will come early and be moderate, and the early chills of fall will only be enough to heighten the dazzling fall colors. Bugs and other garden pests will have been given overseas passports early in the season.

To hold onto these dreams, it always helps to have a couple of stunning beauties showing their stuff out in the chilled bare winter garden.

Iris unguicularis, the winter or Algerian iris, has been blooming since early December. The tender beauty of the blooms and the extraordinary markings on their petals can stop you in your tracks. How can this soft tenderness bloom in such cold and wet circumstances? The question becomes mute after a few seasons with this plant in your garden.

As you might suspect, Algerian iris comes from Algeria, or Turkey, or any other surrounding rocky Mediterranean landscape. There is a variety, *Iris unguicularis ssp. cretensis*, which is unique to the isle of Crete. What they all have in common is a rocky, soil-poor environment, no water from April to October, and intense heat. So, how does one replicate this sort of environment in the cool, damp Puget Sound region?

It can be done. Surely you have a sunny, dry spot in your garden. Perhaps it is in a part of your garden that you do not often tend, or maybe it is surrounded by yard-waste recycling or other bins. The experts recommend planting against the foundation on the south side of the house. The key element for success is to have the plant in a very sunny and dry situation.

That is a summation of the conventional wisdom. You can spend hours on the web and find all this information, and then a lot more, some of which is totally erroneous, a lot of it quite fascinating. So why do I bother to replicate or summarize? A friend called it "filtering literacy." Perhaps that is a bit much, but it does speak to our current TMI situation. Have you found that you can fill up with a lot of credible information, but the need to have it verified or to be reassured by family or friends is a great necessity?

For years I have grown the Algerian iris in my garden. It is planted on a steep hillside (perfect drainage). It is nestled in amongst the rocks and rubble, next to a dry-laid staircase (lime). The site faces south, but is in dappled shade from large overhead tree canopies. The plants are never watered. I cut back the lush foliage to six to nine inches in late October so that I can see the blooms when they start in early December. Do the plants look hacked at? Yes, but if I don't cut back the exuberant foliage, I cannot see the blooms from my living room windows during the cold, bleak days of December and January. And the new growth that accompanies the blooms soon softens the harsh, late fall pruning.

I once saw a sweet crystal vase filled with the iris blooms. It was good to know that someone had also found success with this plant. However, I wasn't so keen on the bouquet. I prefer to have a single bloom in a vase. The markings are fascinating to study—and again, the solitary nature of the display speaks to the beauty that exists within the starkness of this season.

January 2014

Strategizing Color

MY SNOWDROPS ARE BLOOMING!

These first harbingers of spring always delight me with their tenderness and tenacity. Alas, the roses are showing new growth before they have had their yearly pruning.

I cut big sprays from a daphne bush to perfume my living room, along with my paper-white narcissus, which are wildly flopping over their containers, and filling my rooms with their sweet blooms.

I spotted a young, first crocus bloom yesterday. Its small, intense yellow signaled the door to spring is slightly ajar. Such contrasts abound these days, as spring sneaks up on us. The light is thin, the air is still chilly, and when will the cold blast and snow arrive?

Most of the garden seems bare, damp, forlorn, with little appeal to the senses. However, to temper the gloom, think of our fellow citizens, some not very far away (Spokane, anyone?), who can only relate to their gardens by the depth of the snowfall.

Here, we can plant gardens that will delight our senses at this time of year. The thing to remember, as you think about changing your garden for next January, is that the plants need to be in that small area of the garden you move through on these chilly days—beside the mailbox, or by the front entry gate, or close to the porch.

These delights might range from the tree-size *Hamamelis mollis*, to shrubs such as camellias, daphnes, viburnums, and vines, including *Jasminum nudiflorum* and the perennial hellebores.

For me, the bulbs of choice always include the snowdrop and the crocus.

January 1994

Thawing

HURRIEDLY RUSHING OUT in the cold morning air to retrieve my newspaper, I try to *not* look at the shriveled leaves on the shrubs in my garden. Very brief glimpses bring such utter despair. Thoughts of installing concrete paving over the garden beds flit past my mind.

Later in the day, as the weak sunshine lights up some areas, and the leaves unfurl from their nighttime tightness, some glimmers of hope return—maybe all will survive this latest and long-frozen insult from Mother Nature.

I do know that it will be months from now before I can take a final tally. Plants, when left to their own devices, can be much sturdier and stronger than we ever give them credit for. Indeed, it is hard to leave well enough alone, but I encourage you to wait many months before giving up on a poorly looking soul. Their time frame for adjusting and renewing themselves may not be in sync with our aesthetic timetables, but many times they have rewarded me for my patience.

Of greater concern than the mushy perennials, which can easily be replanted, is the health and structural integrity of our large shrubs and all of our trees.

At this time, we may not be able to see any obvious damage, but as the months roll along, do keep an eye out for possible failures. Note particularly if there is any heaving of soil around their bases. Eyeball them for any signs of listing. When it is much warmer, take the time to carefully examine their branching patterns and structures. Our gardens this past year have been subjected to a broad range of stressful weather, and this is the time to assess all the impacts.

If the trees and shrubs appear to be structurally sound, but look poorly in an aesthetic sense, then do wait for them to produce their own recovery.

However, I will stress again that a certified arborist's opinion should be sought for any possible structural problem. Last year, I filed a claim with my insurance company for damages caused by a fallen tree limb. The loss was not greater than my deductible, so the claim was denied. However, in the denial letter, there were several lengthy paragraphs about my duties as a policy holder: "These duties include, but are not limited to, protecting the property from further damage; making reasonable repairs to protect the property...".

If you suspect that the winds, or the excessive rains, or the lengthy freezing and accompanying snow might have weakened your large trees and shrubs, then the cost of a consultation with a certified arborist will seem insignificant if you need to file a claim with your insurance company. The arborist's written report will clearly indicate that you have shown due diligence.

January 2007

January Challenges

I LIKE SNOW, but am just not crazy about ice, or the wind gusts when our trees are "anchored" in very soggy soil. I can only hope that your gardens were not ravaged by the January storms.

I saw a beautifully pruned forsythia bush in bloom yesterday. What a beautiful surprise after days upon days of black, white, and gray landscapes. The bush was a gorgeous glob of sunshine. Often it seems impossible to sing the praises of a tawdry, ubiquitous shrub, such as the forsythia, but there are moments when its vibrant, yellow blooms in January can send your heart soaring with dreams about the floriferous seasons ahead.

Also, when the snow and ice finally melted, my hellebore blooms were nodding shyly downward. How do they survive these ice baths without turning to mush?

Despite the cold and muddy soils, soon it will be time to plant our peas—both sweet and edible. While it appears to still be the deepest, darkest January, we need to get ready for the traditional date for planting peas—Washington's birthday. That means clearing out the winter detritus from our gardens. Jeez, it is all so soggy.

For those of you that do not have or want a trellis structure, please know that you can let sweet peas just trail along over a wall or through a planting bed. It is quite fun to watch the plants entwine themselves within, and over, other plants.

Sometimes you need to cut their ensnaring tendrils back, before they smother a precious bloom or herb, but they are not thugs, and their blooms need to be in a small vase or vases throughout your home. Over the years, I have become quite fond of the variety called "Old Spice." The blooms are softly modest, but their scent is pure bliss. And they need to be picked every other day in order to continue their blooms. Instead of a chore, look at their needs as a wonderful way to draw you out into your garden. By the time of their blooms, your garden will be filled with so much excitement.

You will want to be there.

January 2012

A Pause for the Big Questions

"MIDWINTER SPRING IS ITS OWN SEASON," according to Mr. T.S. Eliot.

The beauty of our January thaw has been breathtaking, with the snow-capped mountains appearing to be just an arm's length away.

There is a bittersweet aspect to our sun-filled days as we read of the devastation from the rains in California, and the massive destruction an earthquake caused in Kobe, Japan, Seattle's sister city. Landscapes give birth to terror, as well as the kindly optimism and excitement portrayed in the seed and plant catalogues arriving daily.

Out in the garden, the sun warms my back as I stoop to pull weeds. I look at the dark, rich soil, and question why this patch of ground is staying put, at least for now. I muse and wonder and find the soil to be distinctly cold in comparison with the warmth of the sun on my back.

I begin to imagine new growth filling in the bare places, which seem to loom so large in the winter garden. I review in my mind the plethora of marked pages in the catalogues, and begin to see there might be some limits that should be imposed on that list of "must haves." I stand up and am caught by surprise at the length of my shadow in front of me, and then I remember it is still winter, in spite of the sun's warmth.

I look at the bare trees and their beautiful traceries against the sky, and note with gratitude the tenacity and loveliness of the first bell-shaped snowdrops emerging from the dank soil.

And I feel a renewed strength for when my thoughts turn again to the big questions.

January 1995

Fresh Starts

THIS PAST WEEK'S INVERSION weather was either good for the winter garden cleanup program, or a guilty pleasure for those rushing off to do some hiking or skiing above the fog. Word got out that there was warm sunshine on Tiger Mountain.

For those that missed the hiking and skiing, the garden did bring some surprisingly great enchantment. The early spring bulbs have thrust their tips through the cold, clammy soil. Gathering up wads of last autumn's sodden leaves, the soil looks fresh and ready for the new season. I still have a layer of mulch from last year covering the bare soil, but it has greatly diminished in scale. There is just enough there to keep my footprints from making mud. And I will have to call my favorite arborist to find out when he can deliver a fresh load of his chips.

There are still mysteries regarding the extent of plant damage from the Christmas snowstorm. It will be many weeks, even possibly a few months, before we will know the full extent of the damage. All around town, I see huge flax plants that are crumpled down. I wonder if there is life at the core of the plant? Just cleaning up the lifeless leaves is going to be a huge chore—and then what?

It will be an ongoing question for spring. Time spent cutting back and cleaning up may reveal that there is no there there. I have a twenty-foot long row of rosemary that cascades over a wall. It is very gray-brown right now. With the wonderfully balmy sunshine on Sunday, I was able to study at length the desolate plants, trying to discern if there was any hope of seeing fresh, green growth. Sadly, the jury is still out, but I want to continue with hopeful optimism. Much like hopefully waiting for my 201K to return to its healthier 401K status.

Many of my semi-deciduous ferns were beaten down to the ground, but the new, tightly-furled fronds looked very plump and healthy. Additionally, this was one of the first years I got to the job of tidying up the old fronds before the new growth started to unfurl. It makes the job so much easier, when the new growth does not get in the way of the pruners!

The *Daphne odora* shrubs are just about ready to throw open their sweetly scented blooms. The snowstorm decimated the early blooms on the *Daphne bholua* shrub, so I have not yet tired of its early spring fragrance. And I spied a fully-formed snowdrop flower, which is a true harbinger of spring in our gardens. The big and lengthy, end-of-year snow and ice storms seem like ancient history now. Fresh spring growth is happening out there in that cold and dim January light.

January 2009

Walking the Talk

THE INSTRUCTIONS for my new worm bin make it seem that I will be the co-creator of the richest soil known to humankind, sooner than I can believe. Similarly, the instructions that came with my Felco sharpening blade make me want to gather up all the poor, blunted pruning tools retired to the garage, and get to work on making them into finely honed instruments again.

However, I must wait to get started on these exciting new projects, and take some of my own medicine first.

I've written before on the need to ensure our public pathways running by our gardens are free from slippery, wet leaves, and overhanging branches. On my walk around our Queen Anne neighborhood on New Year's Day, I saw a great deal of autumnal debris on the ground. Adding insult to near-injury, several times I had to take evasive action in order to avoid being smacked in the face by a low-hanging branch. On two occasions, I had to detour from sidewalk to roadway to get around overflowing plant growth.

And so, I continued on homeward, contemplating how to write of these concerns without sounding too preachy when, lo and behold, I watched a woman get caught up in the thorns of my prolific rose bushes right in front of my gate.

It's a cold and chilly task, pruning these rose bushes between rains; however, the garden looks much better with its winter cleanup, and I see that the buds on the bare branches are starting to fatten. And passage past our gate is now unobstructed.

January 1996

Winter Edible Gardens in the Northwest?

EDIBLE LANDSCAPING at this time of year?

I have yet to find a recipe for bare branches, colorful and artful scaling bark, leathering evergreen leaves or needles, or newly emerging catkins. The leaves of the Christmas rose, *Helleborus niger,* are poisonous, so one might conclude that for certain occasions they could be added to a stew, but wisdom prevails, and we add the dried bay leaf and oregano instead.

Out in the herb garden, the rosemary bush is still strong and upright, despite snows or freezes and relentless rains. Pick a few branches to bring indoors for your windowsill. The fragrance will delight, and the herb will be readily available for your cooking needs.

In a skillet, slowly warm good olive oil, then add the rosemary leaves. Keep this mixture at a low-medium heat for about ten minutes, then remove the pan from the heat and lift out the rosemary leaves. Pour the remaining oil over the baked potatoes, or the meat, chicken, or fish, or add to the pasta sauce.

For the other herbs in your garden that are currently dormant, dig up a piece of the root and bring it indoors in a small pot. Soon, fresh shoots will appear that can be used for your seasonings. This is particularly effective for mints, thyme, and marjoram.

Finally, as the small spring bulbs start to flower, take a lesson from the French. Gather the flowers with the bulbs still attached, and bring them to your table, either with the soil still in place or completely washed off to show the fleshy, white roots. This sort of flower arrangement lasts far longer than cutting the flowers from the bulb.

After the flowers have started to fade, the bulbs can be returned to the garden for the process of allowing the leaves to dry off, in order to re-nourish the bulbs for next year. This treatment is successful for the crocus, *Scilla, Chionodoxa,* and *Muscari* (grape hyacinth) bulbs.

However, bulbs such as daffodils and early tulips will not respond well to this sort of handling, as far as producing for next year. But the daffodil and tulip flowers will remain fresher longer if the bulbs are still attached when you make your flower arrangements.

January 1996

Plant Catalogue: a Confectioner's Shop

THE NEW YEAR is well underway, and gardeners are deeply ensconced in dreamy interpretations of how and where all the gorgeous plants pictured in the beautiful catalogues will enhance and electrify their garden designs.

We have all been let loose in the world's best confectioner's shop. This is also the time of year when the bare bones of the garden are clearly visible.

Is there an edge that seems weak or without form? Does the overgrown English laurel hedge seem grossly out of scale? Is there a plant that could be used to create a hedgerow instead of taking on the expense of a fence?

To create an evergreen structure that will enhance and define the spatial dimensions of a garden area, I have often used *Arbutus unedo*, the strawberry tree. It is evergreen, with beautiful, two-inch long panicles of urn-shaped flowers, and bright, red-orange berries which arrive in late summer. It does well in full sun or partial shade, and can withstand drought or tolerate irrigation. It is a cousin of our native madrona tree, but has none of the madrona's rigorous horticultural requirements, nor does it have what some call a messy habit of dropping leathery leaves and peeling bark.

While its common name suggests a tree-like form, it can be pruned successfully to the appropriate size for an urban home garden.

Japanese maple trees look great with *Arbutus unedo* as a backdrop, and sourwood trees, *Oxydendrum arboreum*, positively glow when nestled amongst or within such a hedgerow.

I am trying to suggest that all those fabulous and expensive plants in the catalogues will bring much greater pleasure if they have a well-defined structure to be placed ever so carefully within.

January 1997

Winter Revelations

SURPRISINGLY, THERE IS A LOT of fussing to be done in the garden these days.

In the moments between storms, seize your secateurs and a rake, bundle up with a good warm coat and hat, and grab a small bucket or basket.

No doubt, thanks to our winter winds, there will be many stray branches and other detritus to be gathered. Soggy leaves and evergreen needles are piled up in corners. The lawn can be gently raked, and you will be amazed at the amount of litter you'll uncover.

Tread lightly on the wet soil, and do not think, yet, about doing any heavy digging, for the soil is too wet.

Stop and admire the tenacity of the newly emerging bulb foliage. The open bareness of the garden reveals its structure. Make quick notes about how it looks to you. Mark with a simple piece of twine or ribbon those shrubs or trees that need to be moved, removed, or thoroughly pruned next month, or after they flower.

Light pruning of crisscrossing branches will add to the sense of bringing order to this winter view of your garden.

Finally, take rough measurements of your garden layout quickly. Back inside, these measurements can be used to make rough diagrams that will be enormously helpful, as you continue to dream, and order from all the plant catalogues.

Also, these rough diagrams are the place to start from when thinking about this year's garden renovation projects, including a deck extension, larger rose beds, and smaller vegetable beds. Much becomes clear in winter; it is a good time to get reacquainted with our garden's bare-boned anatomy.

January 1996

The Crocus: a Shy Harbinger

THESE LAST FEW WEEKS I have been craving salads. The kind made with fresh and tender leafy greens, a few handfuls of sliced roasted almonds, dressed with olive oil, ground pepper, and shaved Parmigiano Reggiano cheese. Quite curious, don't you think? Especially since the currently available lettuce is both expensive and tough.

Finally, the penny dropped after reading one of our Northwest weather guru's blogs stating that this is the warmest January on record. So, obviously I was ready to harvest and dine on those sweet, early lettuces in my garden. The weather may be balmy for January, but alas, the soil is still too cold for any lettuce-seed germination.

However, the early spring bulbs are in full force. The snowdrops are at their supreme moment, and I keep looking for my anemones, but I think it is still a bit too early. The little tufts of the early crocuses are beginning to hold the promise of some blooms, and the buds on our trees and shrubs are fattening up quite nicely.

Many of you will wonder why I am even thinking about crocuses, for they bloom in March or April. These crocuses are forms of Crocus vernus, most often referred to as Dutch crocus. These big, plump, profligately blooming bulbs are treasured by many gardeners for their strong colors and robust blooms, which seem impervious to strong rains and winds. At the time of their bloom, the sun is higher in the sky, and so the chance of the blooms being open and strutting their stuff is greatly enhanced.

The crocuses are the ones now poking their greens above the soil line, tentatively throwing up a tightly furled bloom, which will only open if the sun shines upon it. Again, for these first, shy harbingers of spring, you need to plant them close to where you travel through your garden on these chilly, low-lit winter days. To see the bloom unfolded during a sunny may make you pause amid the gray winter gloom. In that pause, you actually notice the sunshine, and feel the warmth coming back.

The differences between the various species crocus (and what are commonly called the Dutch crocus) are great. You do not want to plant them together, for the difference in their scale is not complementary. The crocus is similar to the snowdrop in that they need to be planted en masse. And there is a lovely tradition from Great Britain to plant crocuses in great sweeps in the lawn.

The usual suspects—squirrels, gophers, moles, and mice—will happily devour your corms. You can use some chicken wire to enclose the corms when you plant them, or just plant many, many corms and watch the action. Crocuses need very good drainage, so you need to add grit or gravel if you position them in a mucky environment. Given that they are tasty treats for the critters I must share my garden with, I shy away from using them—except in a big pot by my front door, which holds a special Japanese maple tree, and out on top of a rubble wall just a few steps from the front door.

I only use species crocus. The tree is bare now, and I can see the small tufts of green and the small blooms. Out on top of the wall, the space is bare because the Epimediums have not burst forth, nor have the ferns unfolded their fronds for this year. In both places the corms have been left untouched!

I mix up all my favorite species corms because they all share a similar scale. My favorite one is Crocus chrysanthus 'Zwanenburg Bronze'. What a fine name, and the bronze markings on the orange-yellow petals are quite handsome. My other favorites include Crocus angustifolius, a bright-yellow bloom with bronze-purple markings on the outer petals; Crocus chrysanthus 'Cream Beauty', with its ever-so-soft cream color pierced by the intense orange of the stamens; and finally, every gardener needs Crocus chrysanthus 'E.

A. Bowles', in order to honor his lifelong dedication to the species crocus. After thirty years he produced a pure, white seedling of Crocus sieberi.

Truly, a fine lesson in patience.

February 2010

The Art of Camouflage

AS YOUR MIND'S EYE TRAVELS back and forth between pretty plant pictures in the books and catalogues, to the neighbor's eyesore you are determined to hide this year, remember that a principle of camouflage is interruption.

Planting one or two trees or shrubs, and then directing the eye down to the earth, will better achieve your goals than erecting a solid plane of a fence or hedgerow. By directing the eye downwards to an intricately designed herb bed, or a complex arrangement of small plants with special rocks, or an elegantly designed water feature with either moving water or specialized water-loving plants, the offending feature in the distance will seem to disappear.

Additionally, I think it is human nature for people to become focused on areas where great effort has been expended. For example, the precisely laid-out rows of a vegetable garden draw the immediate attention of the visitor. It also becomes a place of focus for the gardener who has created it, and renders the undesirable element beyond the garden's border unimportant.

February 1995

What the Snow Tells

LIGHT SNOW BEAUTIFULLY delineates the structure of our gardens. It's almost like having a perfectly executed topographical map of our gardens handed to us for study.

The effects of the wind are clearly shown in the small drifts, while the protected areas show remarkably less accumulation. The garden structures, including paths, fences, walls, bird baths, lamp posts, and mailboxes, create geometric shapes that add abundant contrasts to the plant forms.

The whiteness causes the eye to travel beyond our garden borders to encompass all of the surrounding landscape. I look at the edges of all of our property lines—suddenly they've become minor elements in the whitened scene. We are encompassed by a snowy landscape that embraces us all.

Perhaps that's the charm that so mesmerizes us when we awaken to a day of fresh snowfall. As for prospective damage to our gardens, only time and weather will tell us the outcome.

Currently, the snow is working as a fine protective mulch. If we endure a series of thaws and recurrent freezes, high winds and sharp, cold sun, the damage could be considerable. I prefer to think that we had the good fortune to experience a gentle and beautiful, snowy winter scene that has delighted the eye and informed us of our garden's topography.

I hope for the good rains to come and the promise of a beautiful spring as the light continues to fill our lengthening days.

February 1995

Stark Contrasts

BY SUNDAY MORNING, the havoc wreaked by Saturday's big windstorm was just a distant memory for most of us. Woe to those in the region left without power, but surprisingly, there were few outages, considering the strength and length of the storm.

The quietness that descended on the region late Saturday night was utter bliss. I reveled in the new silence. I wanted no distracting noises, either from the kitchen machines, the TV, or any other sound system in the house. Even a shower seemed too noisy. It was time for a long, quiet Saturday night bath to soothe my badly jangled nerves.

Early Sunday morning, with great trepidation, I ventured forth to assess the storm damage in the garden. What a sorry mess. The garden looked as though it had been hashed in a Cuisinart. Bits of madrona leaves, twigs, sticks, and branches were strewn throughout the paths and beds. Birch twigs, rhododendron leaves, pine cones, and needles were littered about and piled into corners. Any green left on the trees and shrubs was severely frayed along the edges.

Yet, I rejoiced at the sturdy plants—none were lying on their sides. And I found one beautiful snowdrop in bloom, my beacon of hope and renewal.

Hurrying to join some out-of-town friends for a late breakfast at the Pike Place Market downtown, I was amazed at the number of people out and about on a Sunday morning. While the air was cool, the warmth of the sunlight was divine. I should have found my sunglasses, wherever they might be. Of course, we were all out and about—the light was golden, something we haven't experienced for weeks. Just possibly, our green, fuzzy, and mossy aura might disappear.

Aside from the ubiquitous "Go Seahawks" cries of Super Bowl Sunday, there was another theme party going on up and down the streets. People of all ages were stretching their limbs, strolling with their faces to the light, joining in small groups to exchange smiles and laughter. After months of banging each other with our umbrellas as we scurried along, backs hunched against the foul weather, we immediately relaxed into a celebratory mood. I have seen this phenomenon before—perhaps unique to the Northwest?—where we immediately seize upon the beauty of the fair weather.

A few hours later, I went out to get the fixings for a Sunday supper. The sun was still shining, the air temperature was noticeably warmer than the morning hours, but the streets were empty. You could shoot the proverbial cannon down Queen Anne Avenue and hit nothing. It felt like there had been a huge evacuation.

The game must have started.

February 2006

Winter: Staying Connected

I DUG UP A CLUMP of my snowdrops and brought them inside. They're still surrounded by soil in a glass vase, with some rocks and moss dressing at the top of the arrangement.

By having them inside, they remind me to look at their cousins as I zip through my sodden garden early in the morning. They have replaced the narcissus bulbs, which put on a grand display of growth and scent, but finally fell out of their containers.

The demureness of the snowdrops makes for very pleasant company as I peruse the many gardening catalogues arriving daily. They remind me to be modest in my ordering frenzy.

You may want to try this indoor arrangement with some of your crocus bulbs. There is a wonderful earthiness involved when you dig the bulbs and bring them inside. It becomes a way to stay connected to the garden, even in wet weather.

With our mild winter, the buds are fattening now on our trees and shrubs. It's time to make sure that last year's detritus has been thoroughly cleaned up, including all the corners, crevices, and whatever hides beneath low-growing plants.

The herbaceous borders should be thoroughly cut back, in order to see the new growth emerging. This is a good time to plant new lily bulbs in your perennial borders.

The temperatures are mild, so it is a good time to be in the garden. Try to keep your projects small and compact so that, when the rains come, you can easily gather up your tools and head back inside to your catalogue ordering projects.

February 1994

February's Heatwave

FINALLY, THE FIRST CROCUS joins the blooming snowdrops. The narrow leaves were up, and I could see a bloom stem, but it always takes sunshine to force open the blooms on these species crocuses. Close to my front door, there is a large pot holding a Japanese maple tree, and this becomes the perfect place to plant these diminutive early spring bloomers.

The species I most prefer is *Crocus chrysanthus,* and I mix three varieties: 'Cream Beauty,' 'Gypsy Girl,' and 'Zwanenburg Bronze.' This is a subtle mixture of clear, yellow flowers with assorted maroon and bronze markings. Not a spot of purple, violet-blue, pink, or white will be found, for the outer landscape is still mostly tawny in color, except for the white and maroon of the nearby *Daphne odorata var. marginata.* The spring pinks, whites, and soft hues of blue will arrive next month, along with the surrounding, tender green of the unfurling fern fronds.

Late last week, I watched several of my friends totally rearrange their overly complex schedules. Suddenly there were new dental appointments, some heart-breaking tales of family needs, and other dire situations that required them to take time off from their jobs. Why the frenzied, slightly nefarious actions? Well, the weather reports indicated spring-like temperatures in the fifties.

Earlier in the week, it was possible to feel a slight lessening of the chill to the air. One wondered—is this the February moment? All gardeners talk about this phenomenon that happens every February, but never at the same time, so it is impossible to schedule ahead. I recently checked my ongoing garden journal, and found that it can happen as early as February 4, and as late as the end of the month.

After months (it often feels like years) of watching our chilled and frosty gardens from afar, we suddenly have a few days of relatively balmy weather. We rush out to till the soil, plant our sweet peas, check on all the emerging daylilies, daffodil and tulip shoots, and quickly plunge our noses into the witch hazel blooms. There is so much to observe and to do.

Of course, there are vast, soggy drifts of winter detritus in the corners, or caught up against fence posts and shrubs. There is a sense of making it all right again as we clean and clip back stray bits. We pause at the bare spots, and make mental notes about how it could look ever so much better. Basically, though, we are just swept away with being back in our gardens. So much to do and so little time. And we blissfully forget that this little heat wave will end. If we were to look at our calendars, there is still the dynamic month of March ahead, with all its fierce, cold winds, sleet, possibly snow, but definitely rain.

Such a tease, this February pause.

February 2008

Softening the Final Design

AS YOU RETHINK and refine this year's garden design during these rainy days, remember to include in your plans the areas that you'll need for the actual work of making and running a garden.

Paths should be, ideally, at least three feet wide, and planting beds that are wider than four feet need to have within them places to stand for you to do the weeding, dead-heading, staking, or picking the blooms. Otherwise, you'll need good access from the other side of the planting bed.

At this time of year, it is so difficult to remember the fullness of summer's growth, but that fullness will hide and soften our needed working constructs. Planting beds less than five feet in depth always look constrained and cramped after the plants have started to mature.

In my driveway, for example, I needed a place to step out of the car, but I have hidden this stepping area within a planting bed, so that from afar the area appears generous in its size. The ground-cover plants come right up to the edge of the car's wheelbase, which makes the parking area appear lush with vegetation.

Before constructing the garden's hard surfaces, it's good to spend a year with these areas just covered with 5/8-inch crushed gravel. During that year it is possible to learn how and where plants can be used to soften the final design.

Usually, the hard-surface area can be made smaller in the process, which can ultimately reduce the cost. The gravel can later be used to improve drainage in sodden areas, work as scree for an alpine garden, or as fill material for dry-laid rock walls.

February 1994

Renewing Our Connections

THE AIR HAS CHANGED from its brittle winter cloak. There is a softening. And the light has definitely returned, even on our incessantly cloudy days. It is indeed safe to sing out the cliché: "spring is in the air."

We revel in the brief hours of sunshine, much as we do later in the year on those first days of summer heat. We are reconnecting to the outer world, throwing off our hibernation tendencies. It is exhilarating to feel in our bones the surge of renewal.

The garden is challenging us once again. The early crocuses have thrown out their little bristly shoots, with some showing off their first, sunshine-yellow blooms. The snowdrops are pure whiteness. The Algerian iris (*Iris unguicularis*) finally decided to bloom last week. There have been years when their first blooms occurred in early December.

What is different? Is it less baking sunshine due to more shade from the surrounding trees? Do they need to be lifted and divided? Was it too cool last summer? Yes, the garden always offers us many conundrums to ponder.

Then there are the stacks of seed packets waiting to be attended to. The sweet peas and the early snow peas can now be directly sowed into the ground. It still remains surprising to me that these seeds do not rot away in the cold, dank soil. It takes a complete leap of faith every year for me to get them into the ground in February.

Most of the other seeds will be sown indoors in a few days or weeks, or sown directly into the ground during March, April, or May. While I don't always follow my best intentions, I have found that a big planting-time chart has helped with getting the maximum successes out of my seed packets.

Yes, we know that "xyz" needs to be planted in mid-April, but on my planting chart I stake out a day or two, and with a bright red, wide-stroke marker, I add those days to my chart. Then there can be little procrastination, and I can clearly show my schedule to those well-meaning others who may be infringing on my time.

Yes, one might or could call it "extreme" gardening, but those seedlings, when sprouted, only reinforce your cleverness at getting them underway this season.

One other brief bit of insight: look ahead at the to-do lists that are published showing the monthly garden activities. Some of the "chores" listed can in fact be done sooner, rather than later. Of course, there is a wonderful smugness that comes from getting ahead of the game. However, do remember that the garden will bring you to your knees and teach you humility, no matter how great your ingenuity.

Hopefully, our notes from previous years, and especially last year, will guide us towards appropriate choices for further plantings. Where are the bare spots? Where are the overgrown or ugly shrubs that need replacing? Should we add more trees? To the last question I always say, yes. For me the trees in my garden are my soulmates. They steadfastly renew themselves after being pummeled or severely injured by storms.

One year, my mighty madrona tree tore itself apart and, in the process, also wiped out one-third of a mighty red maple. They both showed great discretion by not injuring anyone or any structures. That same year, my husband injured some of his own limbs, and I suffered the indignities of some surgeries. Those two trees became icons out in the garden for me. Yes, we were injured, as the trees had been, but the trees were still standing tall and just a little bit reconfigured. We could do the same.

February 2013

Like Early Spring

Fog

The fog comes
on little cat feet.

It sits looking
over harbor and city
on silent haunches
and then moves on.

—Carl Sandburg

WITH THE WEATHER REMAINING so very calm, wet, and mild, a feeling of early spring is settling in around us, just as in Carl Sandburg's perfect description of fog.

The snowdrops extend their reach, the early crocuses also grow taller, and both have been joined by the emerging blooms of witch hazels, daphnes, edgeworthia, camellias, bergenias, early azaleas, forsythia, and heathers.

The forsythia shrubs are now only seen in older, somewhat abandoned gardens. The shrub form does not enchant the eye, but the yellow blooms, at their peak, become golden orbs of sunshine in these low-lit, late winter days. As the older gardens become transformed by new owners, the shrub will continue to become an even scarcer element in our landscapes, until some dedicated hybridizers will go to work with their talents and produce exciting and exotic cultivars. This has happened to the old-fashioned bergenia plant.

I grew up with the plain *Bergenia cordifolia*. The leaves were coarse and leathery, and often thoroughly chewed by snails, cutworms, or root weevils. The leaves lay flat to the ground, and in the early spring a few clusters of non-descript pink flowers would rise above the dull, green leaves.

Now the hybridizers have produced an exciting new array of bergenia cultivars. The 'Purpurea' selection produces magenta flowers on tall, magenta-colored stems, and the leaves can be flushed with purple tones in the summer, changing to red in autumn, and then in winter a burnished, purple color. A newer cultivar, *Rosa* 'Zeiten' has soft, pink flowers set off by the bronzy, winter foliage.

A few years ago, I discovered *Bergenia emeiensis* with its tall sprays of large, pure-white flowers rising above the slightly bronze, paddle-shaped leaves. There is nothing dull or "thuggish" about this elegant plant. What a surprise, for I really had come to loathe and totally dismiss anything called bergenia. Now I am planting *Bergenia* 'Eric Smith', known for its upright and striking foliage. I have interspersed these plants with the six-foot tall, summer, Oriental lilies. May exotica reign supreme with this "old-fashioned" plant while we await the hybridizers' work on the forsythia shrub.

Another awkward spring shrub is *Hamamelis*, known as witch hazel. However, this shrub has exceptional fall color, and again it has been extensively hybridized, so that its fragrant, early spring, spider-like flowers now come in a full assortment of red, coppery-orange, and yellow colors. The fragrance is wonderfully elusive in contrast to the thundering perfume of the *Daphne odora* shrub. My small daphne shrub makes itself known these days, sixty feet from my front gate! It speaks to the full scents that will be coming later in the year. Yes, it will get warmer, and there will be the joy of that first, full-scented rose.

Meanwhile, the camellias are stuffed with blooms. Often, with this incessantly damp, rainy weather, the blooms turn brown with rot. This can be avoided by removing all but one bud in each grouping. The English are famous for their beautiful groves of camellias in their woodland gardens. They always debud their plants in the fall. It always surprises me that this horticultural practice is so little-known here in the States. Once you have had a season with rot-free camellia flowers, the tedium of the job in the fall is erased.

As the almost-spring garden continues to unfold and enchant us with its treasures, the time has come to start the vegetable seeds indoors. All this unfurling and unfolding going on around us really starts to erase from memory the cold emptiness of deep winter.

February 2010

Time for Patience

THAT COLD SNAP WREAKED havoc in our gardens, but ultimately it may have been great news. "What?" you holler, as you peruse the frayed remains of your favorite plants.

For the last three or four years, we have not had any truly severe winter weather. This has allowed the chewing insect population to thrive, and the drifting spores of mildew to multiply. A good, hard freeze reduces the population count of these garden visitors. We've had the freeze now, but the aesthetics leave much to be desired.

And this is the time for the hard decisions. Will that plant recover? And what about those over there? It will be weeks, and in some cases months, before the verdicts are in. Meanwhile, resist the urge to prune back the "dead" parts. The plants have been stressed, and pruning them will add to their discomfort at this time. And the long-range forecast includes more cold snaps.

To make the sorry mess a little bit more palatable, this is a good time to straighten the edges. With a sturdy metal rake, my favorite being the California Flexrake, clean out the mud and weeds from your sidewalk gutter. For the tap-rooted weeds, such as dandelion, hack at them with a shovel. Cleaning up this debris is a great way to stay warm, and believe me, the tidy aesthetics really will make you feel better about your garden, and your neighborhood.

Also, it is a great way to catch up early on local gossip. We have all been indoors too long now, hiding away from our neighbors. It is time to get out and greet each other again. Do remember to give a big warm smile and a vigorous wave to the really tiresome ones!

In the garden itself, clean the windblown winter detritus of leaves out of the corners. Along the paths, clean up the muck lurking under the plants and pull out those early spring weeds. Give your lawn areas new, sharp, clean edges. All of this fussing and tidying will make you feel quite virtuous, and truly help you to overcome some of your dismay over any freeze damage. It will also give you more time later for attending all those April plant sales.

Now, however, we need that elusive quality called patience, so we can just squelch our current disappointments, and soldier on through the predictable blasts of cold that March makes us endure.

March 2006

In March: Stepping Lightly

WHILE WE STILL HAVE TO DEAL with the capriciousness of March, our lawns need their first mowing. Surprisingly, this can be done now in spite of the recent, heavy rains. Let the lawn dry for twenty-four hours, then set the blades high on the mower so that there will be no chance of stirring up any mud.

Edging the lawn is effortless, thanks to the damp soil, and I have been delighted with the relative ease involved in removing all of the big taproots on the dandelions. The established garden beds need to have the detritus from winter storms cleaned away, including any storm-damaged branches on the plants, and a fresh layer of mulch applied as a deterrent to spring weeds.

The growth is starting on the roses, so if they still need pruning, now is the time.

Also, finish any major pruning to large shrubs and trees, except the spring-flowering varieties. The time can be shortened out in the garden when foul weather looms, but these preliminary forays into your projects can give you a wonderful head start.

Pay careful attention to your work with the soil, for it can easily become compacted at this time of year. When planting, be sure to amend the soil with compost, and always recultivate the soil area where you have stood.

This is the season for stepping lightly in the garden.

March 1995

Also, in March: a Test of Endurance

THE CROCUSES HAVE ARRIVED in their modest, close-to-the-ground splendor.

The sun that broke through last weekend made its March debut. These past few days, the wind came out of the cold north and made time in the garden a chilly affair.

Last Sunday I performed the ritual of planting peas and, of course, more trees. When I came indoors my teeth ached from the windchill.

March is a month that can test the endurance of any strong-willed gardener. The promise of the fullness of the seasons ahead begins to percolate in the veins, but the struggle with the cold wind, and wet, heavy soil is the immediate challenge. The increase of light is like the cavalry riding out the woods to save, or at least lengthen, the day.

The sun glinting off Puget Sound and the snow-capped mountains east and west; the fattening buds on our trees and shrubs, and the tender shoots of the bulbs, reinforce a sense of promise.

March 1994

Sun!

OH! WHAT A WEEKEND FOR the die-hard gardener. Sun on Saturday and an uncommon warmth on Sunday afternoon. At the same time, I was amazed at the sturdy crop of dandelion-like weeds flourishing in my planting beds. However, these broadleaf pups just sailed out of our damp soil with one good prod from my favorite, worn-down screwdriver.

The roses are in full-steam-ahead mode, and yet it is not too late to prune them. Roses need to have an open shape, so cut off any canes that are crossing others, and prune inside canes to force the growth outward.

Along with a good, sunny location in the garden, roses need to have good air circulation passing through their growth. As the first panic of "so much to do" hit this weekend, it was wonderful to be back in the garden with all the tender, new growth on the cusp of spring.

March 1994

Spring Vagaries

JUST WHEN YOU THOUGHT it was safe to plant out those leggy seedlings, big, fat, fluffy snowflakes filled the skies and whitened the ground. Fortunately, by midday, all was slush rather than frozen solid. It was that exquisitely balmy day last week that promised us an end to winter's nasty coldness. Ha!

Some follow-up remarks are needed regarding my recent tree and shrub planting advice. It is important to establish a watering basin of some sort for the new plant. It is important to remember to position it at the outer edge of the plant's drip-line, because that is the area where new roots will be developing. If the water basin is positioned just at the trunk, the problem of rot and drought occurring at the same time is highly probable. So, perhaps we need a new term—maybe "water ring"—because basin suggests a bowl-shaped depression, which would have the water running towards the trunk of the tree.

A water ring would force water out away from the trunk and towards the areas where new roots are developing. Those roots are so important for anchoring the tree. Which leads to the contentious issue of whether trees need to be staked.

Actually, it is quite fun to read many differing opinions, almost all of which are presented passionately, by both amateurs and professionals. After tiring of the controversy, and feeling guilty when I staked and when I didn't stake, I now leave it to common sense. If the tree has a poorly developed root system, I lash it to a stake or stakes, and then slowly release it to the winds over a two-year period.

If the tree is planted in a wind corridor, it gets staked during its youth. If the slope is steep, staking will be required. And so forth.

I remember my father staking his trees. Those trees were lashed ever so tightly to his beautiful stakes. Before the stake was hammered into the ground it had been sanded and buffed to perfection. He always used redwood or cedar. And then slowly and methodically, over several years, he would release the trees from his protection. Towards the end of his life he knew that he would never see their grandeur as mature trees, but he still planted as many saplings as he could, wherever possible.

In my garden I have five of his saplings, now looking like grown-up trees. Of course, I always worry, when the winds are gusting, that maybe I removed the stakes too soon.

So far, all is well.

March 2009

Acknowledgements

While writing her columns for the *Queen Anne & Magnolia News* for more than two decades, Madeleine Wilde worked with a number of exceptionally talented editors. Among them were Jack Arends, Maggie Larrick, and Richard Jameson. Each of them established their own, unique connection with Madeleine and her writing.

A sincere thank you goes out to Lynn Sousa, Mike Frappier, Grigory Nechipruk, and Alan Taylor for their helping hands in Madeleine's garden.

And a thank you to Duane Dietz, ASLA, for his time and attention.

Last, and not least: A bow to Phil Bevis and Annie Brulé and the rest of the team at Chatwin Books—inspired, deeply informed makers of beautiful books and a pleasure to work with.

Mike Dillon and David Streatfield

About the Contributors

MADELEINE WILDE was born in Pasadena, Calif. in 1943 and grew up in the Bay Area. After earning her bachelor's degree in social science at the University of California at Santa Barbara, she became a computer programmer in New York City.

In the early 1970s, back in the Bay Area, she immersed herself in the world of garden design and building.

Madeleine moved to Seattle in the late 1970s. In 1986 she and her partner and future husband, David Streatfield, bought an old house on Queen Anne Hill's southwest slope. They began work on the creation of their garden in 1993, a project which lasted several years. Madeleine started writing "Notes from the Garden" for the *Queen Anne & Magnolia News* in the early 1990s.

In that same decade she served on the Queen Anne Community Council and the Pike Place Market Historical Commission, and later served on the Northwest Horticultural Society Board. In her later years, Madeleine was a committed volunteer for Ballard Food Bank.

Madeleine died at her Queen Anne home on February 16, 2018, just shy of her seventy-fifth birthday.

MIKE DILLON, former publisher at Pacific Publishing Co., is the author of five books of poetry and three books of haiku. He grew up on Bainbridge Island and lives in nearby Indianola on the Kitsap Peninsula.

His journalism has won numerous awards over the years; in 2013 the Washington Newspaper Publishers Association recognized him with its Master Editor/ Publisher award. His essays and poetry appear in journals in this country and abroad. His most recent book is *Departures: Poetry and Prose on the Removal of Bainbridge Island's Japanese Americans After Pearl Harbor,* from Unsolicited Press (2019).

DAVID STREATFIELD is a noted historian of West Coast landscape architecture and professor emeritus in the department of Landscape Architecture at the University of Washington, where he taught from 1971 to 2012.

Born and raised in England, Prof. Streatfield received his Diploma in Architecture at Brighton College of Arts and Crafts in Brighton, England in 1956. He earned a Certificate in Landscape Architecture at University College, University of London in 1962, and his Master of Landscape Architecture at the University of Pennsylvania in 1966.

His book, *California Gardens: Creating a New Eden* (Abbeville Press 1994) was chosen by the American Horticultural Society, on the occasion of its seventy-fifth anniversary in 1998, as one of the seventy-five "greatest American garden books in 75 years."